# A HOUSE OF PRAYER

## PRAYER MINISTRIES IN YOUR CHURCH

COMPILED BY
# JOHN FRANKLIN

LifeWay Press®
Nashville, Tennessee

ISBN 0-7673-9393-7
Dewey Decimal Classification: 248.32
Subject Heading: PRAYER

This book is a resource in the Adult Leadership and Skill Development diploma plan of the Christian Growth Study Plan.
Course LS-0034

Scripture quotations identified as NASB are taken from the NEW AMERICAN STANDARD BIBLE,
© Copyright The Lockman Foundation, 1960, 1962, 1963, 1968, 1971, 1972, 1973, 1975, 1977, 1995.
Used by permission.

Scripture quotations identified as NIV are from the Holy Bible, New International Version,
copyright © 1973, 1978, 1984 by International Bible Society.

Scripture quotations identified as KJV are from the King James Version of the Bible.

Scripture quotations in the appendix are from the New King James Version.
Copyright © 1979, 1980, 1982, Thomas Nelson, Inc., Publishers.

To order additional copies of this resource: WRITE LifeWay Church Resources Customer Service;
One LifeWay Plaza; Nashville, TN 37234-0113; FAX order to (615) 251-5933; PHONE (800) 458-2772;
E-MAIL to *customerservice@lifeway.com*; ORDER ONLINE at *www.lifeway.com*;
or VISIT the LifeWay Christian Store serving you.

*Printed in the United States of America*

Leadership and Adult Publishing
LifeWay Church Resources
One LifeWay Plaza
Nashville, Tennessee 37234-0175

# TABLE of CONTENTS

# WRITERS

## THE COMPILER

**John Franklin** serves in the Pastoral Ministries Department at LifeWay Christian Resources with responsibilities for prayer. John coauthored *Spiritual Warfare: Biblical Truth for Victory* as well as contributing to articles on prayer for various publications.

John received degrees from Samford University, Southern Baptist Theological Seminary, and Beeson Divinity School where he received a doctorate in teaching leaders how to lead a prayer meeting. John and his wife Kathy have three children, Daniel, Nathan, and Susanna. They live in Nashville, Tennessee.

## THE CONTRIBUTORS

**Greg Frizzell** serves as the director of prayer and spiritual awakening for the Baptist General Convention of Oklahoma in Oklahoma City, Oklahoma. He has written several books on various prayer topics.

**Elaine Helms** serves as the prayer evangelism associate for the North American Mission Board. She has served as the prayer coordinator for Johnson Ferry Baptist Church, a megachurch in the Atlanta area. She has also produced books on intercessory prayer and for many years has spoken at various conferences on that subject.

**T. W. Hunt** served as the prayer consultant for LifeWay Christian Resources until his retirement. He is still a sought-after speaker on prayer and spirituality, based on his best-selling discipleship courses, *Disciple's Prayer Life, In God's Presence, The Mind of Christ,* and *From Heaven's View.* Perhaps his greatest distinction is the life of prayer he exemplifies.

**Phil Miglioratti** served as a pastor for many years until he dedicated himself full-time to heading the National Pastors Prayer Network, an organization he founded. Additionally, he serves on the National Prayer Committee, speaks on prayer subjects at various conferences, and leads a prayer emphasis for an association of over 1,000 churches.

# The BASICS of PRAYER

## T. W. HUNT

Many years ago I typed all of the prayers of the Bible into the computer. Because the Bible is the Christian's reference tool and guide for life, I wanted to know what it says about prayer and how the saints in the Bible practiced prayer. We can be humbly grateful that the Bible records, for our instruction, successes as well as failures in prayer. Ever since I compiled these references, I have taught people that the basic way we relate to God is through prayer.

Prayer is a relationship with God. Our basic relationship with God is as child to Father. Jesus taught us to use the title *Father,* and the early church adopted the term (see Rom. 8:15; Gal. 4:6). Because Jesus also used the familiar term *Abba* to refer to the Father, I sometimes call Him Daddy. This title seems to establish firmly the nature of our relationship with Him. Hebrews 2:11 tells us we can call Jesus Brother. I always say, "High and Holy Brother," considering His exalted nature. In John 15:15 Jesus authorized us to call Him Friend. It is also permissible to call Him Bridegroom (see Matt. 25:1).

God likes for us to relate to Him in a way that brings that relationship to our consciousness, whether it is a title for Him; a title for us, such as *child of God;* or a quality in Him or us that reveals the relationship. God created us for Himself. Without that relationship no life has the ultimate meaning God designed our lives to have. Jesus said, "I can of mine own self do nothing" (John 5:30, KJV). Everything He said or did grew from His relationship with His Father. We need to be related to the Lord Jesus in the same way He related to His Father. Our relationship with the Father is through Jesus by means of the Holy Spirit. We cannot take one breath without Him, for "in Him all things hold together" (Col. 1:17, NASB). We are expressing that relationship whenever we talk to Him who is always with us.

## Why Should We Pray?

The first reason we pray is that the Bible commands it. First Thessalonians 5:17 tells us to "pray without ceasing" (KJV). A Christian assimilates spiritual armor through prayer (see Eph. 6:10-18). The Bible gives repeated examples of great saints whose regular practice was prayer. The Bible records more than five hundred examples of prayer. It contains more than four hundred additional passages on prayer or teachings on prayer. In other words, almost one thousand passages deal with prayer in one way or another.

Second, Jesus commanded us to ask (see Matt. 7:7-11; Luke 11:9-13; John 14—16). Our authority, the Bible, and our supreme authority, the Lord Jesus, make prayer a priority. Prayer must be one of the basic pillars on which the church builds its work. It is evident that God wants us to pray.

## How Do We Pray?

The words, attitudes, and methods we use in prayer are important, for they reveal much about our heart and our beliefs about the One to whom we pray.

### Pray According to God's Character
When we pray, it is God's plans we are concerned with. After all, Kingdom work was His idea. He is the one who includes us. All prayer must be consistent with God's character. God is always consistent with Himself; His works are consistent with His character. This means that when He answers prayer, He is consistent with what He has always been. Our aim is to bring ourselves—and therefore our prayers—in line with His aims.

We cannot want God's aims until we have a healthy respect for them. Jeremiah, Isaiah, and Paul all feared the Lord. Several years ago I realized that I did not respect the aims of the Lord because I did not fear Him—at least not the way David and Jeremiah did. Today we are taught not to fear. Fear is considered a defect. But in the Bible fear is an asset. Those who feared the Lord had their prayers answered, because fear aligned them with God's purposes.

Therefore, I always begin my longer prayers (not my unpremeditated "arrow prayers," which I shoot to God throughout the day as occasions arise) by meditating on God's attributes or at least by reminding myself of the basics—His unspeakable holiness, His unlimited power, His all-wisdom, His infinite knowledge, His unmatchable love, and all that is God. When I do this, the Spirit of God enables me to fear Him properly. No one knows for sure exactly what God may or may not want to do in a specific situation. However, we can realize the mind of Christ (see 1 Cor. 2:16). We approach prayer with humility and reverence because we are not all-knowing and all-wise.

I have discovered a safety measure to help me move from the known to the unknown. I always begin my prayers by naming some of God's qualities as revealed in His Word. Always begin with the known qualities of God. This does not mean that we are not to ask; we are repeatedly commanded to ask. But do not begin with the asking. Begin with God's holiness, power, transcendence, and glory or the qualities that will concern our later asking—His immanence, knowledge (He knows more about our concerns than we do), mercy, and longsuffering.

Beginning our prayers in this manner places our mental state and our spirit where the mental state and Spirit of God are—within God's nature and purposes. When I follow this procedure, I often begin to see God's purposes in the various causes I am praying for. At all times God sees an incredibly big picture. He sees consequences we have no way of suspecting. He sees His kingdom advancing in clear detail we cannot imagine. My purpose is to have the mind of Christ to a degree that I will think as He thinks about the people and purposes of my prayer. And proceeding from the known—God's attributes—to the unknown—God's will in a specific situation—helps me achieve my purpose. It will help you, too.

### Be Holy
A second factor in prayer is inner cleanness. We must be pure in order to approach a holy God. God's holiness is absolute. It cannot be violated. Although believers can be holy through Jesus Christ, our holiness can be violated by sin. The slightest sin is a dreadful offense to God's awesome holiness. The psalmist tells us, "If I regard iniquity in my heart, the Lord will not hear me" (Ps. 66:18, KJV).

Satan is never satisfied with one sin. He always wants us to commit more, so he accuses us (see Rev. 12:10), and we run from God. The result is that our sin compounds itself. Creation has been in a state of ever-increasing decay since Adam's first sin. Even science agrees that the universe is in a state of entropy. After the fall all sin has contributed to the decay of creation. Sin violates the original order of creation, and that is why it is so important to Satan. He wants us to join him in his rebellion, which is where we were before our salvation. When we run from God after we sin, we join Satan's rebellion against God. This does not mean that we lose our salvation, but sin has serious consequences for our prayer, because prayer is fellowship with absolute holiness. Only holiness can fellowship with holiness.

Therefore, ideally, we must strive to avoid any sin. Sin brings to a dead stop the process of sanctification in us, the process by which we are made holy. When we slip and fall, we are unholy, and sanctification cannot continue. To restore the process of sanctification and to avoid compounding our sin, we should confess sin the instant we realize that we have slipped. This has been referred to as being confessed up-to-date, but actually, we should be confessed up to the minute.

We have the trustworthy word of God that "if we confess our sins, he is faithful and just to forgive us our sins" (1 John 1:9, KJV). The Greek word for *confess* means *to speak the same thing* or *to agree.* I always tell God when I sin, "Father, what I just did is not like You, and it's not like the real me."

You may think that "the real you" is the "you" that committed the sin. Humanism teaches that we are products of the past. Christianity teaches that we are products of the future. Therefore, when I say "the real me," I mean the "me" that God is in the process of making. From God's standpoint, I have not yet arrived. With much Bible study and a little imagination, I can appreciate the splendid perfection that I will be at the end of the process. So I agree with what God is making of me rather than what I was in the past. Confess immediately. Never delay.

If Satan is never satisfied with our sin, we can be assured that God is satisfied with Christ's righteousness in us. That is His name—"the Lord our righteousness" (Jer. 23:6, KJV). We can confidently approach God because He sees Christ in us, and that is perfect holiness.

## Be Humble

A third factor in effective praying is humility. Humility is the only personal attribute that can look up to God. Like love, humility cannot seek its own good. Only humility seeks the greater good, the good that God sees in the big picture, and only humility knows how to accept God's will. Rebellion against God's desire is a telltale sign of pride. If I begin prayer with God's attributes, humility falls into place. James 4:10 tells us that we can humble ourselves. We do that most definitely by reminding ourselves of who God is. We must know who He is

before we can pray. Throughout the Bible God demonstrates over and over that He prefers the lowly: the younger son Jacob, the shepherd David, the peasant girl Mary. If we can shuck off the trappings of our common human failing of pride, we can capture God's attention.

## Be Sincere

A fourth factor in effective praying is sincerity (see Jas. 5:17). God pays no attention to anything that is not real. For this reason many of history's famous pray-ers, like Rees Howells, have found that a powerful help to effective praying is identifying with the person or the cause you are praying for. Christ identified with us when He became human. When we identify with others, we follow Christ's example and are better able to identify with Him.

One way to identify with others is to try to imagine how they feel as they go through their crisis or problem. Then place that identification within the realm of God's love, protection, and care for the entire family, group, church, or world. This means that you are willing to suffer if that occasion arises. If you pray for the hungry, try fasting. If you pray for the poor, try dressing more modestly. Being in their place brings fervency to our prayers, which is pleasing to God.

## Be Fervent

Fervency is closely related to sincerity. The church that prayed for Peter in prison was fervent (see Acts 12:5). Fervency is not an emotion we can manufacture. It is a by-product of the Holy Spirit's presence. We must be filled with the Holy Spirit (see Eph. 5:18). I always ask God to give me the Holy Spirit in all that is me—my spirit, my emotions, and my mind. Then I consciously depend on the Spirit's direction.

## Pray in Faith

A final factor Christians often ignore in their prayer lives is faith. Hope and faith are closely related, but they are not quite the same thing. Hope is the present enjoyment of a future blessing. We don't have the desired object yet, but we can relish its coming. Faith, on the other hand, is simply understanding God's goodness. When we understand how much God wants to give, which usually requires much

Bible study, we gladly accept His gifts. Hope brings the future into the present; faith takes the present into the future.

An obstacle to faith is dwelling on the past. Christianity always places the emphasis on the future. Christians are in the process of becoming. What we are becoming is God's business, but it is far grander than we presently imagine. Our prayers need not be eloquent since God isn't impressed by our eloquence, but they do need to be engrossed in His great love and the exciting things He wants us, our friends, and our church to become.

## What Kinds of Prayer Can We Use?

Prayer begins the Christian life as we pray to receive Christ. The Bible gives six other kinds of prayer that properly relate us to God after our salvation experience:

1. Confession
2. Worship
3. Praise
4. Thanksgiving
5. Personal petition
6. Intercession for others

Confession of our sin restores us to fellowship with God. We also confess as we agree with God about His nature and about His intention for us and His world. Worship is expressing to God our adoration of Him. Praise is elevating God's attributes. Thanksgiving is expressing gratitude to God for His provision and blessings. Personal petition is one kind of asking. Intercession for others is another very important kind of asking.

Confession, worship, praise, thanksgiving, and even personal petition are all important prayers because they are biblical ways to achieve God's purposes. Yet the main work of a church's prayer ministry is intercession. If you follow the procedures outlined above, you will practice all kinds of prayer. You cannot approach Him without confessing your sins. You cannot properly relate to Him without worship. You cannot know Him without praise. And thanksgiving is participating in His riches, which are a part of Him. But the harder work of prayer is intercession.

### The Vital Role of Intercession

The kind of prayer we fail at most often is intercession for others. If numbers count, the Bible contains about the same number of prayers of intercession as prayers of praise—the two most frequently found prayers in the Bible. More importantly, it contains more teaching on asking (petition and intercession) than any other kind of prayer. Isaiah, Paul, and Jesus taught on asking prayer.

Years ago as I typed all of the prayers of the Bible into the computer, I noticed that every time God wanted to do a major work in the Bible, He raised up an intercessor:

- When God wanted to deliver the children of Israel from Egyptian bondage, He raised up Moses. The Bible records 12 great intercessory prayers by Moses (see Ex. 32:11-14,31-32; 33:12-23; 34:5-9; Num. 6:24-26; 12:4-16; 14:13-24; 16:15,22-24,41-50; 21:7; Deut. 9:25-29).
- When God wanted to deliver the Jews from the murderous plot of Haman, He raised up Esther, who fasted for her people (see Esth. 4:16).
- When God wanted to restore the Israelites to their Jerusalem home, He raised up Nehemiah, who prayed effectively (see Neh. 1:5-11; 4:4-5).
- When God wanted to bless the churches, He raised up Paul, whose prayers demonstrate immense spirituality. His letters contain 25 great prayers, all of profoundly spiritual intent (see Eph. 1:15-21; 3:14-21; Phil. 1:9-11; almost all introductions and closings to Paul's letters).

One day as I was typing, I suddenly realized that God does not usually work alone. I confess that I do not fully understand this, for I know that God does not need any of us. He can do whatever He pleases without consulting anybody. He is God. The unspeakably powerful works of creation and redemption were accomplished without our help or advice. So why did He create us and redeem us? Not for any lack or need in His own character but simply from His incomprehensible love. Love created and redeemed in order to love even more. We were created and redeemed not from His need but from His love. God created us for fellowship with Himself. That fellowship can be realized only through prayer.

It is the expression of our relationship with God.

That same incredible fact underlies the reason God works the way He does. He does not need our help; He could do whatever He wishes with no assistance from us. And yet His unbounded love wishes us to be involved in His work in this universe. To comprehend this, think of an earthly father. He can do his work without his child, but he wants his child's fellowship as he works. God wants us to include us in directing His vast creation. Persons in the Bible were included in God's work, and God has not changed. We are not merely His instruments; we are His partners in the Kingdom enterprise (see 1 Cor. 3:9). Prayer expresses our partnership with God. It is God's way of involving us in His plans, His work, and His enterprises.

In intercession we join the war against Satan. Because God cares for us, we must care about Him and His work. Satan fights intercession because He does not want to see God's work advancing. He distracts us, causing us to get tired or unconcerned. The fact that we are commanded to resist these impediments (see Jas. 4:7) indicates that they can and must be resisted.

### The Results of Intercession

The first accomplishment of skilled intercession is that it places the intercessor in the position Christ Himself is in. Christ intercedes for us in heaven (see Heb. 7:25), and He intercedes for persons we pray for. Our job is to know His mind. We can know His mind if we constantly depend on Him, study His life, and appeal to the Spirit to lead us that way. Sometimes I pray about an object for weeks before I am able to discern the mind of Christ. But persistence pays off, and ultimately, I begin to feel confident in knowing the mind of the Lord.

The second accomplishment of intercession is that it secures the work of God. God could perfectly well do His work without our prayers, but that is not the way He likes to do it. A love so vast and inclusive that it will not work apart from the participating work of His beloved is inconceivable to us. But can you imagine what working with God does for us (see 2 Cor. 6:1)? It leads us first into identification with His purposes and then into identification with God Himself. It gives real meaning to—

"your kingdom come,
your will be done
   on earth as it is in heaven" (Matt. 6:10, NIV).

The more we work with God through prayer, the more fervently we can pray the Model Prayer. In it we are moving in heavenly circles.

## Who Should Pray?

Every believer is commanded to pray. How strange that God wants to hear from us! It is a compelling thought. The command in the Great Commission is to "make disciples," not just converts (Matt. 28:19, NIV). No growth can occur if we are not in continuous contact with God. Prayer is our breath. We cannot hold our breath for long periods of time; rather, we constantly continue breathing, just as any normal growth is constant. Natural growth, by definition, cannot be intermittent. The same is true of spiritual growth. The Holy Spirit is with us to help our continuous, constant prayer.

Certainly, the church staff ought to pray. Most of us can usually tell when a sermon has been prepared without prayer. A lack of prayer also shows in the other work of the church, too—in the letters we receive, in the music we sing, and in the lessons we teach or study. The church is, after all, to be a "house of prayer" (Matt. 21:13, KJV).

Graciously, the Lord also calls a special group of people to the intense prayer work of the church, which is the prayer ministry. This call may not be a mountaintop experience, but these Christians know their responsibility in the prayer ministry through the work of the Holy Spirit. If a person clearly understands that the Kingdom will be brought only through prayer and is a praying person himself, that person is a likely candidate for the prayer ministry. It is not the church's most glamorous work; it is not the church's most public work; but it is the church's most effective work.

## What Should We Pray For?

Every believer has the responsibility to pray for certain areas of concern.

### Pray for the Church Staff

The most obvious prayer burden a prayer ministry can assume is prayer for the pastor and staff. We can pray for their health and for their spiritual growth. We should pray for the pastor's sermons and his direction of the church's ministry. Specific situations also need attention, such as crises or problems staff members may encounter. In one church the pastor and each minister submit to the prayer ministry their immediate needs for the month, and the prayer ministry prays specifically for them. This, of course, also involves the pray-er in the church's total ministry.

### Pray for Special Requests

If a church's prayer ministry becomes well known, it receives large numbers of prayer requests. Often these involve sickness or death. Sometimes they involve special crises—a wayward child, a troubled marriage, a family disagreement. We must always pray for the mind of Christ in such situations. Although these can become painful prayers, we must identify with Christ. If an individual is troubled, we feel his or her pain, just as Christ does. If a young person experiences uncertainty about a call to full-time Christian service, we can project ourselves into his or her future ministry. Special crises involve very difficult but very important praying.

### Pray for the Church's Ministries

We need to pray for the current work of the church— Sunday School, Discipleship Training, Woman's Missionary Union, Music Ministry, women's ministry, men's ministry, outreach, children's ministry, and youth ministry. We are now training our young people for the most difficult period in Christian history. We must prepare them for a world that is increasingly secular, godless, materialistic, and competitive. They desperately need our hardworking prayers.

### Pray for Long-Range Plans

We can pray for our church's long-range plans, which should include massive evangelism. Perhaps the church's plans include a building program. Prayer for the lost is one of the most important prayers we can pray. Long-range plans should be God-sized. Prayer is learning to think God-sized thoughts. Much of our long-range vision can originate only in prayer.

### Pray for Missions

A major part of our praying should be for missions. The worldwide missions effort is greater than it has ever been in the history of Christianity. In some parts of the world, such as South Korea and East Africa, people are turning to the Lord in massive numbers. In other parts of the world the plowing is slow and difficult. Both the International Mission Board and the North American Mission Board offer valuable aids to prayer for missions. Both offer a monthly bulletin with current prayer concerns. They also have toll-free numbers by which interested pray-ers can get recent information.[1]

We should pray for missionaries' language mastery. Pray that God will protect them from harm and from Satan. Pray that they will not become ill with various illnesses that plague some parts of the world. Above all, pray that they can be effective witnesses and make disciples. I always pray these prayers for missionaries on their birthdays.

### Pray for Persecuted Christians

A very needed and neglected prayer is for the persecuted church. More people have died for their Christian faith in the 20th century than in all previous centuries combined. In Muslim countries, in Communist countries, and in some Orthodox countries the persecution is intense. These Christians need many kinds of prayer. Pray for their protection. Pray for the missionaries called to work in these difficult areas. Ask the Lord to provide Bibles for struggling Christians. Be much in prayer for effective witnesses and ask the Lord to protect them in their activities. Missionaries even need help in getting visas and work permits. As I read newspapers and magazines, I watch for specific names of victimized Christians.

## Why Should We Pray Together?

The most authoritative prayer available to the body of Christ is unified prayer. One of the greatest miracles in the Bible occurred when four men prayed together. Nebuchadnezzar had threatened to kill the wise men (astrologers) if they did not tell him what he had dreamed and the meaning of his dream. When Daniel, Hananiah, Mishael, and Azariah (Shadrach, Meshach, and Abednego) prayed together in desperation (see Dan. 2:17-19), God revealed both the dream and its meaning to Daniel. Herod imprisoned Peter intending to execute him, but the church fervently prayed together (see Acts 12:5), and an angel delivered Peter from prison, another outstanding miracle in answer to united prayer.

## The Authority of United Prayer

I grew up in a very devout home that had a daily family altar, so I grew up seeing many answers to united prayer. I committed that when I was married, we would have a family altar in our home. About a year before I got married, my fiancée, Laverne, and I agreed to meet daily for prayer and Bible reading. That way it was easy to enter marriage with the practice already established.

Over the years we have seen many answers to our joint prayers and have always enjoyed that time together. However, in 1983 the Lord had plans to deepen our prayers. Laverne's mother died of cancer at the age of 44. Laverne's father was one of four brothers and sisters, all of whom developed cancer at the age of 57. Because of this background we feared that Laverne would also develop cancer. Early in 1983 a lump was detected in her right breast. However, after the mammogram the doctors in radiology failed to see the lump, so we enjoyed a carefree summer. We later learned that she still had cancer and that it had continued to grow while we were confident it was not there. By the time a biopsy revealed its presence in November, the cancer had spread into her lymph system.

After hearing that devastating revelation, I prayed almost continuously for weeks before the Lord directed Laverne and me to study 2 Corinthians. This is one of three books in the Bible that address suffering, along with Job and 1 Peter, plus a brief mention in James and several references by Jesus. Every evening after dinner we would sit together with the Bible in our hands. Slowly, word by word, verse by verse, we carefully worked our way through that profound book.

As we did so, God began to knit our spirits together on a scale we had never known before. God even granted several miracles, but the greatest miracle of all was what God did between us. One Tuesday evening after Laverne had finished her chemotherapy, we asked God to show us what we had learned through the experience. We realized then that the

closer the bond you present to God when you pray together, the greater the authority God invests in your prayer. In other words, the closer the bond, the more powerful the prayer.

## The Power of United Prayer

We find this pattern throughout the Book of Acts. Shortly after Pentecost when Peter and John had faced the Sanhedrin, the church prayed, and "the place where they had gathered together was shaken, and they were all filled with the Holy Spirit and began to speak the word of God with boldness" (Acts 4:31, NASB). Surely they were remembering Jesus' promise: " 'Again I say to you, that if two of you agree on earth about anything that they may ask, it shall be done for them by My Father who is in heaven. For where two or three have gathered together in My name, I am there in their midst' " (Matt. 18:19-20, NASB).

The most convincing proof of the power of unity in prayer is found in Acts 1:14: "These all [the eleven apostles] *with one mind* were continually devoting themselves to prayer, along with the women, and Mary the mother of Jesus, and with His brothers" (NASB, italics added). The result of that unified prayer was the greatest miracle in the Book of Acts—Pentecost. The outpouring of the Holy Spirit on New Testament believers came when a small group of believers united in prayer in an upper room. God grant that somehow we may recapture that unity and that our times may see another Pentecost!

## Joining God in Prayer

Throughout Bible times God established the precedent of making His work also the work of His people. We have seen examples of His use of intercessory prayer to bring about His purposes—Moses, Esther, Nehemiah, and Paul. The Bible names many others—Jacob, David, and Hezekiah, for example. The calling to be an intercessor is, biblically, one of the greatest callings God gives. We don't earn the title; it comes from God's purposes as revealed in His Word.

God's two greatest works of all time, creation and redemption, were accomplished without prayer from His people. We weren't there to "consult" when God created the world. We did not have the wisdom to ask Him to die on the cross for us. Prior to the cross, all efforts toward salvation were directed to human works. But the biblical evidence indicates that God's basic way of running this universe is through the intercession of His saints. Intercession is working with God (see 2 Cor. 6:1). Therefore, we need to be very serious about doing His work His way. His way is a high, holy, and difficult way. Satan fights intercession more than anything else we do. Having practiced intercession for many years, I realize that asking you to do it is asking for hard work on your part. But intercession is the noblest work God entrusts to us humans. In prayer we fully realize our relationship with God, and with that we assume the nobility He intended humans to have from the time we were created.

---

[1]International Mission Board, (800) 395-PRAY (7729). In Richmond, Virginia, 355-6581. North American Mission Board, (800) 554-PRAY (7729).

# STARTING *A* PRAYER MINISTRY

## JOHN FRANKLIN

### How the Saints of God Started Ministries

If you want to start a prayer ministry God's way, what should you do? That is the only question that matters, because God will not bless anything initiated in the flesh. So instead of writing solely from my experience, I researched the Bible to study how the saints of God started their ministries. (I am loosely using the term *ministry* to mean an organized activity that built up the saints and advanced God's kingdom.) Interestingly, I discovered that there was no single way it happened. The majority of the saints, like Moses, were summoned at God's initiative. Some, like Nehemiah, had the activity in their hearts and asked God if they could do it. Others, like Hezekiah, were in positions of authority and simply began to act. Some, like Esther and Daniel, took advantage of opportunities. However, two common denominators exist among these patterns.

1. The success of their ministries was based on the quality of their relationships with God, not their methods, techniques, or organizational abilities.

2. They always told others what God was saying, and God worked in others' hearts to confirm that

it was He. Sometimes that process was quick, and sometimes it took years, but they faithfully continued to bear witness to God's will until others responded.

So a successful prayer ministry does not depend on a formula. However, this does not mean that we should not suggest a plan. Remember, God worked with the majority in a particular way. So I would like to suggest six steps churches can follow to start a prayer ministry. These logical steps are consistent with the ways of God. Be prepared, however, if God wants to do something unconventional in your case. Your relationship with Him will determine how you know the difference.

Study the chart on pages 14–15 to overview the six steps and to get the big picture before reading about the steps in depth. Within some steps I will address the unique differences between a pastor's and a layperson's roles in starting a prayer ministry. If you are on a church staff, you will primarily follow the pastor's track, but in some cases your role will be a hybrid, especially in step 1. Whatever your situation, reading both tracks will provide a greater understanding of how staff and laity should relate in launching a prayer ministry.

## STEPS FOR STARTING A PRAYER MINISTRY

| PROCESS | If you are | Step 1 LAY THE FOUNDATION | Step 2 CHOOSE THE LEADERS | Step 3 ESTABLISH THREE PRINCIPLES | Step 4 LAUNCH THE MINISTRY | Step 5 DEVELOP A RENEWAL STRATEGY | Step 6 DEVELOP A LONG-RANGE STRATEGY |
|---|---|---|---|---|---|---|---|
| MAIN GOAL | Pastor | Awaken and motivate the church to pray. | | | Cast the vision from the pulpit. | | |
| | Both | | | Agree on priorities. | | Keep the service to God fresh. | Create strategies for internal and external impact. |
| | Layperson | Secure pastoral support. | Recruit a Barnabas and team. | | Prepare for the launch. | | |
| SUBSTEPS | Pastor | • Cultivate a growing personal prayer life. • Motivate for a successful prayer ministry. • Utilize three arenas to awaken and motivate. | • Evaluate whom God is calling. • Tie accountability to God. • Recruit the team. • Understand your role. | | Communicate the importance of prayer. | | |
| | Both | | | • Maintain an inward focus. • Maintain an outward focus. • Let God renew the church's vision. | | • Recruit leaders. • Communicate. • Gather feedback. • Reinforce the importance of prayer. • Celebrate. • Plan annually. • Make budgeting a priority. | • Create an internal strategy for developing a praying church. • Create an external strategy for your church to serve God through prayer. |

## STEPS FOR STARTING A PRAYER MINISTRY

| | | Step 1 LAY THE FOUNDATION | Step 2 CHOOSE THE LEADERS | Step 3 ESTABLISH THREE PRINCIPLES | Step 4 LAUNCH THE MINISTRY | Step 5 DEVELOP A RENEWAL STRATEGY | Step 6 DEVELOP A LONG-RANGE STRATEGY |
|---|---|---|---|---|---|---|---|
| | *If you are* | | | | | | |
| PROCESS | | | | | | | |
| SUBSTEPS | Layperson | • Set up a meeting.<br>• Define roles and make commitments.<br>• Consider ramifications of a lack of support. | • Identify your Barnabas.<br>• Enjoy the benefits.<br>• Evaluate and enlist. | | • Gather feedback.<br>• Choose a program.<br>• Establish a time line.<br>• Promote the program.<br>• Plan the launch Sunday. | | |
| TIME LINE | Both | As much time as it takes to make sure the goals happen | As much time as it takes to make sure these are in place | As quickly as possible, hopefully within a month of choosing the coordinator | Three months or less | In first three months | In first year or two |

## Step 1: Lay the Foundation

**THE PASTOR'S GOAL: TO AWAKEN AND MOTIVATE THE CHURCH TO PRAY**

The primary responsibility for the prayer ministry falls on the shoulders of the pastor. This does not mean that the pastor does all the organizational and administrative functions of the prayer ministry, but it does mean that you have the responsibility to create in your congregation the desire to be a praying people. Admittedly, the work of developing a heart for prayer in your people is much harder than organizing a program. *However, for a prayer ministry to succeed, the hearts of the people must first be tilled so that they want a relationship with God in prayer.* After that has been accomplished, you will be ready to organize something. So how do you lay the foundation for prayer ministry by stirring the hearts of your people?

### Cultivate a Growing Personal Prayer Life

The first step in building a house of prayer begins with your personal prayer life. God works in response to prayer. If you pray for your people, God will honor your request and will stir their hearts to want to pray. Conversely, if you don't pray, there will be dryness in many members' lives. Second, prayer is more caught than taught. When your members see a dynamic prayer life in you, they will want the same thing. Finally, God will not honor hypocrisy. Why would He fulfill your request to do something in the lives of your people that you don't practice yourself?

### Motivate for a Successful Prayer Ministry

How long it takes to motivate your church to pray depends on where members start. If they have no interest in praying, it may take a long time. If the church body is already motivated, then you are ready to move to your next step. Before outlining some practical steps to motivate the church body, I want to emphasize the importance of first preparing hearts. This biblical pattern holds true whether God is about to lead the children of Israel out of Egypt, give the Ten Commandments, install David as king, or fulfill the second coming. He first prepares the hearts of His people to receive what He is about to do. Most pastors who have trouble getting their people to respond to prayer do so because the people haven't been stirred to the point of asking for it.

A clear example of this principle occurs in Luke 3:1-15. Have you ever wondered why God sent John the Baptist? Why didn't He just send His Son? Scripture records that John's life function was to *prepare* the way of the Lord. Evidently, humans are not wired to immediately respond to change and new directives from God. They must first be prepared. Notice that God also allowed circumstances to grab the people's attention. They were in dire straits as a nation. The Romans ruled the country; their leadership was horribly wicked (see Luke 3:1-2); and to top it off, God had not spoken for four hundred years. When God broke the silence through John, it undoubtedly caught everyone's attention. The national conversation suddenly buzzed about spiritual things. Verse 15 makes the effect of John's ministry crystal clear: the people "were waiting expectantly," and they began "wondering in their hearts" (NIV) whether John was the Messiah.

People will not pray just because you start a prayer ministry. In fact, if their hearts haven't been prepared to want one, they will ignore or oppose it.

### Utilize Three Arenas to Awaken and Motivate

How can you increase interest in prayer? Use every opportunity to raise awareness of the role of prayer. The biblical saints always told others what God was saying. As a pastor you can do this in various ways.

*Preaching.* The sermon is traditionally considered the centerpiece of Protestant worship services. You can expound the Scriptures so that church members can understand the importance of prayer and the role it plays in their lives. The Holy Spirit will then convince members of the need to pray.

*Teaching.* Pastors often have various opportunities to teach, such as Sunday night, Wednesday night, and small-group studies. Furthermore, pastors can institute lessons on prayer to be taught in every Sunday School class for two weeks, a month, or longer if desired.

*Other opportunities.* Many avenues, such as drama, the church bulletin, a guest speaker, a prayer conference, and special events such as the National Day of Prayer or See You at the Pole, can raise members' interest in prayer.

Ideas are limited only to your imagination, but the goal is clear. Use every means and opportunity available to create desire and expectation and to raise awareness in your congregation. Several signs should become apparent when God is stirring the people. You may notice that they begin to ask questions, pray more, or display more interest and hunger to pray than they have in the past. Their awareness of the seriousness of sin grows. Their conversations refer more to prayer than previously. God often begins to answer prayer in a more obvious manner to encourage their faith. Someone may even mention that the church needs to start a prayer ministry or that the midweek prayer service needs to focus more on prayer. When things like these happen, you know that God has worked in hearts sufficiently to start the prayer ministry. If you try to launch a prayer ministry when God hasn't stirred the people, it will almost certainly fail.

## THE LAYPERSON'S GOAL: TO SECURE PASTORAL SUPPORT

You must be absolutely convinced of the necessity for pastoral support. No other person in the church has as much influence over the people of God. Anytime a church member receives a burden from the Lord to start a ministry, its success will depend in large measure on the pastor's backing. Since prayer plays such a vital role in the lives of God's people, do everything possible to secure pastoral approval and commitment to see that this ministry thrives.

### Set Up a Meeting to Share Your Dream and Gauge Your Pastor's Heart

Make an appointment so that you will have an uninterrupted time with his undivided attention. Be sure to prepare for the meeting by praying. While sharing with the pastor, gauge his receptivity.

*Be ready to respond if your pastor has a heart for prayer or is favorable to a prayer ministry.* If your pastor has already been asking God to raise up someone to start this ministry, you will both rejoice to learn that you have the same goal. It could be, however, that your pastor is favorable but has simply never thought of organizing a prayer ministry. In this case your job is to explain the benefits of this min-

istry. Also tell your pastor ways God has been working to bring you to the point of approaching him with this idea. Your goal is that he understand God's activity in your life so that he will know your heart.

*Dream with your pastor about the possibilities for the future.* Let him know what you see and ask him as the leader of the church what he sees. Hopefully, this will help both of you see God's vision for prayer ministry in your church.

*Be ready to suggest a concrete plan if the pastor is ready.* For example, if you want to start an intercessory prayer room, talk about where you envision it. You should have already worked through key logistics, such as how to organize requests and how people can enter and exit the prayer room.

Actually sharing a concrete plan will depend on whether the pastor is ready to enact the ideas you have talked about. It may be that he likes the idea of an organized prayer ministry but not the intercessory prayer room. If this is the case, overexuberance could make him hesitate. If, however, he is ready to move, then you will be prepared. The key in knowing whether to suggest a plan is determining whether his heart is ready to do something.

### Define Roles and Make Commitments

When the pastor is ready to move on a definite plan, define your roles and secure several commitments from him. First, his roles will be to stir the congregation and to raise awareness. Your roles will be those of an administrator and a committee leader. Ask him to commit to a sermon series on prayer or to have lessons in Sunday School classes. He may choose one or both. Make sure you communicate that you recognize his leadership and in no way desire to work contrary to his vision for the church. Finally, secure a commitment to budget support for the ministry. If your pastor is not willing to do these things, you may need to consider whether the ministry has a chance of succeeding at this time. Securing these commitments up front will create the best climate for launching the ministry. Also, concessions are easier to obtain on the front end than later.

### Consider Ramifications of a Lack of Support

If the pastor doesn't have a heart for prayer or is unfavorable to the idea of a prayer ministry, the situation is more difficult. All of the potential situations that could occur cannot be addressed here. However, let me list some realities that may help.

Most pastors don't think negatively of prayer. If your pastor doesn't have a heart for prayer, he would probably not oppose or deny your starting a prayer ministry. You just won't receive much support.

If your pastor doesn't have a heart for prayer, a need exists in his life. Perhaps he has never seen God do mighty things, has become discouraged or disoriented, has a broken relationship with God, or is burned out. The first activity you may want to suggest is to organize the church to pray regularly for the pastor. This will support and encourage him. Additionally, when God begins to do things, it will show him what God can do through prayer.

Be careful of your attitude. Don't become frustrated with or think less of your pastor if he doesn't demonstrate a passion to pray. Remember, it is God's responsibility to change your pastor. Your jobs are to be faithful, regardless of how long the process takes, and to maintain a genuine love and respect for your pastor. Sometimes pastors don't react against prayer as much as they react against a person they perceive as having a superior attitude or with whom they have had conflict in the past. Make sure your heart is right toward your pastor and that you clearly convey a right attitude. Finally, be patient. Keep bearing witness during the next few months. Keep praying.

What's the next step if your pastor doesn't respond? Your relationship with God will help you determine your next move, but you can still encourage others to catch a heart for prayer. Your church may not change as fast as you would like, but God will use your faithfulness like leaven. The desire in others will grow little by little as they see your walk before God and ways He answers your prayers. Your faithfulness has the potential of swaying your pastor when he sees the benefits.

## Step 2: Choose the Leaders

> **THE PASTOR'S GOAL: TO IDENTIFY THE LEADER FIRST, THEN THE TEAM**

### Evaluate Whom God Is Calling

How do you identify the layperson God is calling to head up the ministry? God may be using someone who has a heart for prayer to lead others to pray. This person may already be informally leading by encouraging people to pray. God's prior activity through his or her life may indicate that leading a prayer ministry is the next logical step.

If no one is already involved informally, you will need to discover the person who will lead the ministry. Typically, this person will surface after you've started the process of stirring hearts. For example, this person may approach you after a service and express appreciation for what you've said lately about the importance of prayer.

If a leader doesn't surface, you must develop someone to be the leader. Ask God whom He has chosen and seek to enter a mentoring relationship. Depending on your circumstances, the training may occur formally, informally, or both.

Questions you can use to identify a leader for your prayer ministry are listed in the box on page 19.

### Tie Accountability to God

Once you have prayed and determined whom God is calling to lead the prayer ministry, you are ready to approach that person. Usually, it is helpful to share your dream and ask the person to pray about whether God would have him or her lead it. This allows time to think, and it ties accountability ultimately to God when the person senses that the assignment is from Him.

### Recruit the Team

The pastor should keep in mind several considerations when recruiting the team.

*The size of this team will depend on the size of your church.* A team may not be necessary if your church size does not demand it. Because Jesus set an example of having His disciples work in groups of two or more, you should seek at least two laypersons help start the ministry. Most teams should not exceed eight, however, because a larger committee usually becomes cumbersome and slows decision making.

Churches have traditionally used the term *committee* when referring to a working group in the church. A current trend replaces the word *committee* with the word *team* or another designation that doesn't sound so formal. Depending on your church, this may be beneficial.

## EVALUATING SOMEONE GOD IS CALLING TO THE PRAYER MINISTRY

- Is the person in a growing relationship with God? This determines success more than any other qualification. In the long term God will not prosper those who drift or walk in disobedience.
- Does the person have a passion for prayer? This is evidence that God has worked in the person's heart to prepare him or her for this assignment.
- Does the person have integrity? Does the person influence others with his or her life as much as with his or her words?
- Do others in the congregation respect the person? People will not follow those they don't respect.
- Does the person have a calling? Most leaders can articulate a sense of calling. In some cases an individual does not personally sense a call, but the church recognizes God's gifting of that individual.
- Does the person have leadership skills? Ministry requires working well with others; leadership skills are essential. If the person does not have leadership skills, either God is not calling him or her, or He is calling the person, and you must help develop his or her skills.

*Involve your prayer coordinator in the selection process.* Together the two of you will provide a check and balance to make sure you get the right team members. Also, as the team's primary leader, the prayer coordinator needs to be confident of the choices in order to avoid friction.

*The prayer coordinator should do the recruiting, not you.* Typically, people are accountable to those who recruit them. Having the coordinator recruit team members helps the team recognize the authority the church has vested in the coordinator to lead this ministry. Furthermore, this also communicates to your coordinator your vote of confidence in his or her ability to lead.

### Understand Your Role
Invest time with the team on the front end. Starting something new requires more time and attention in the beginning. Attending the initial meetings will help team members understand your spirit and vision. It is also an opportunity to boost your prayer coordinator's ability to lead by publicly recognizing him or her.

Delegate administration and decision making to the team but not the vision. As the pastor, you need to stay in contact with the prayer coordinator to ensure that your ministry philosophy is always in harmony with the team's decisions. Decisions, events, calendar dates, and types of prayer ministries should be delegated, but the coordinator should never be free to function outside the bounds of your vision. If serious conflict arises between their decisions and your vision or if the team is not capable, spend time working with them. Adequately communicate and guide them in a direction that advances your vision.

## THE LAYPERSON'S GOAL: TO RECRUIT A BARNABAS AND TEAM IF NECESSARY

God rarely gave persons in the Bible an assignment to do alone. Jeremiah had Baruch, Paul had Barnabas, and Moses had Aaron. Seek someone you can trust to labor with you.

### Identify Your Barnabas
God may raise up your Barnabas from any number of areas, but Scripture records that God often built relationships and then revealed a Kingdom calling. Sometimes these relationships came from families. For example, Moses and Aaron were brothers; two sets of the apostles were brothers; and David and Joab were cousins, as were Jesus and John the Baptist. Others came from friendships. Andrew and Nathaniel were friends when Jesus called them; Paul and Barnabas knew each other a long time before their first missionary trip; Peter and Andrew were friends with James and John. Don't be surprised if God lays a close friend or relative on your heart.

### Enjoy the Benefits
You may need a team eventually or immediately, but recruiting one person has benefits.
- You will have a soul mate and a prayer partner.

- You will have someone to share the work.
- You will have another ministry perspective.
- If you have a team, your Barnabas can also communicate the vision.

Finally, look for someone who complements your weaknesses. True maturity recognizes personal limitations and is not threatened by others who display greater skills in certain areas.

### Evaluate and Enlist

Read the questions in the box on page 19 as guides for evaluating and enlisting your Barnabas.

## Step 3: Establish Three Principles

**THE PASTOR AND LAYPERSON'S GOAL: TO AGREE ON PRIORITIES**

A minimum of three core values must pervade any prayer ministry for it to prosper. When a prayer ministry gets in trouble, one of these elements is invariably missing or neglected. Therefore, before selecting a prayer team, the pastor and prayer coordinator or the layperson and Barnabas need to make sure that both agree on these three principles. If a key leader doesn't hold to these commitments, the ministry will be forever crippled and ineffectual. You must make sure you are in agreement before proceeding.

Becoming of one mind can occur formally at a meeting in which you agree to talk about the prayer ministry or informally over lunch. You need to give the process of becoming like-minded as much time as needed. If you are not like-minded, the ministry will fail, and the congregation will suffer. Convincing the church family of the importance of prayer will become much harder in the future. It is better not to proceed than to proceed without a commitment to the following three principles.

### Maintain an Inward Focus

Maintain an inward focus on helping church members develop intimate, personal, dynamic relationships with God so that they will clearly understand when God is speaking to them. This element ensures that church members know how to communicate personally with God. People do not grow in a relationship with someone they cannot communicate

with. I believe this is one of the greatest needs in most churches today. After salvation many Christians have not grown in their relationships with God because they have not been taught how to dialogue with Him. The prayer ministry must see this as a priority and seek every means available to help members toward that end.

### Maintain an Outward Focus

Maintain an outward focus on seeking to know where and how God wants to advance His kingdom. Christian maturity comes when saints no longer spend most of prayer time trying to get God to answer their own wants, needs, wishes, or desires. Instead, they seek to know God's purposes, perspective, desires, and wishes, and they labor in prayer and deed toward that end. The prayer ministry should provide opportunities for this type of intercession.

### Let God Renew the Church's Vision

Let God continually renew the church's vision. I once heard a national prayer leader say that the issue is not to get people to pray more. The issue is to help them have a vision from God, because in the Bible all prayer flowed from vision. As I ran my mind through the Scriptures, I realized that this was true. Prayer ministries die whenever people fall into the trap of praying from duty or because it's a good thing. Prayer ministries stay vibrant when people maintain a sense that God has ordained the transformation of their world through prayer and that God will act when they pray. The prayer coordinator's primary responsibility is to make sure the participants keep this truth foremost in their minds.

When the pastor and the prayer coordinator are in harmony, you are ready to launch the ministry.

## Step 4: Launch the Ministry

**THE PASTOR'S GOAL: TO CAST THE VISION FROM THE PULPIT**

The first goal in launching the initial program of your prayer ministry is to create energy by giving members a shared vision of what God does when His saints pray. Major components in casting a vision include preaching, educating, raising awareness, getting feedback, dreaming, and reinforcing the truth about prayer. The administrative tasks are secondary, although vital, for ensuring that the ministry is launched successfully.

## Communicate the Importance of Prayer

The work of stirring the congregation continues now in earnest with the pastor, the prayer coordinator, and the team. The major difference this time is that you want to give what has been simmering in the people's hearts the concrete form of a program. Successfully launching a program is contained in one word: *communicate!* Communication implies a two-way process: your expectations and their feedback. This may be done through the following means.

*A sermon series.* You may choose to do a month-long study on prayer that addresses various biblical truths.

*Sunday School lessons.* The greatest educational arm of the church is Sunday School. Not only does it provide a wonderful opportunity for teaching, but it also allows members to ask questions and give feedback.

*Raising awareness.* Different ways exist to capture the congregation's attention. People have found the following ideas helpful.

- *Testimonies.* Let members share one- to three-minute testimonies on Sunday mornings for several consecutive weeks. This approach is powerful because members testify to what God has done in their lives, thus creating a hunger and an interest in the hearts of other members to experience God in the same way.
- *Drama.* A skit always catches people's attention, and it can communicate the message in ways preaching cannot.
- *Mystery.* Arousing curiosity stirs people as well. For example, suppose your church is celebrating its anniversary and you ask people the major cause of its founding. You may want to give clues for a month about what motivated the first members, culminating in a Sunday when you tell the story of how the church was birthed in a prayer meeting.
- *Humor.* This approach enlivens drama, announcements, or sermons. Humor wins favor with people, making them more receptive.

Be sure to coordinate with the steps the team will be taking. Again, your primary roles will be to highlight the importance of prayer and to support the team's actions.

## THE LAYPERSON'S GOAL: TO PREPARE FOR THE LAUNCH

A great factor in ensuring that the ministry starts right is coordinating planning with the pastor. Lay out the key steps below in a definite time frame and present your strategy to your pastor. When the steps have been agreed on, remind him when they occur. Keeping your pastor informed will help keep him enthusiastic.

### Gather Feedback

If people do not have a chance to give input into a new ministry, they will be less likely to participate in it. After a period of time preaching, educating, and raising awareness, a wise idea would be to create a format for members to ask questions and give input on what the prayer ministry ought to look like. Feedback can be generated in a number of ways, including questionnaires or small-group dialogue. The latter can be accomplished through Sunday School and will probably prove more effective than questionnaires.

Making the effort to solicit feedback results in at least three benefits.

1. Many great ideas come from the congregation.
2. The opportunity for members' personal involvement in shaping the ministry creates a greater likelihood that they will be involved.
3. Feedback will reveal whether God has worked sufficiently in members' hearts to implement a concrete program. If the church doesn't respond favorably, don't launch a program. Instead, go back and continue working with the pastor to help awaken and motivate the congregation.

### Choose a Program

Based on feedback from the congregation and what you sense in prayer, you should choose the prayer program God wants for your church. No two churches are alike. Because God worked in a certain way in one church does not guarantee He will do it in another. You must seek God to learn where He wants you to begin.

### Establish a Time Line
After members know what type of prayer ministry to begin (intercessory prayer room, home prayer cells, prayer chains, etc.), the following items should be discussed several weeks in advance of the launch day.
- The Sunday to launch the ministry
- A calendar of major deadlines that must be met
- Necessary materials to be ordered
- The location for the ministry
- Training dates for volunteers who sign up
- Responsibilities of team members
- Concerns unique to the type of prayer ministry you are launching

### Promote the Program
After people understand the importance of prayer and are motivated, you can promote a specific program. Several ideas for promotion follow.
1. Ideas/opportunities
- *Pulpit announcements.* These prove very effective, come from the pastor, and require little effort.
- *Personal invitation.* The majority of people who get involved do so because someone invites them.
- *Churchwide mailing.* This communicates the importance of the ministry: it means enough to put a letter in every person's hand.
- *Newsletter.* If your church has one, this is another good format.
- *Meetings.* Seek permission to make announcements to various committees. Informing your church leaders is vital.
- *Web site.* If your church has a Web site, use it to announce plans for your prayer ministry.
2. Visibility
- *Banners.* Hang these prominently in the sanctuary.
- *Posters.* Hang these in Sunday School rooms and hallways.
- *Kiosk.* This portable, multimedia promotional stand on wheels can be equipped with a TV, VCR, bulletin board, and/or information holder. Place it in a high-traffic area of the church to make members aware of the prayer ministry.

- *Testimonies.* Enlist members for one- to three-minute testimonies on Sunday mornings.
- *Drama.* Use a skit to catch attention.
- *Mystery.* Draw attention to the prayer ministry by arousing curiosity or using teasers in your promotion.

### Plan the Launch Sunday
When the day finally comes, make sure the following details are in place.
1. *Sign-up system.* Provide a way for volunteers to sign up, as well as a way those absent on launch Sunday can sign up the following Sunday.
2. *Cards.* Send reminder cards to volunteers confirming the date and time of their training.
3. *Training time.* Launching a ministry without training is like sending troops into battle without showing them how to use their weapons. Training provides indispensable advantages, such as equipping volunteers to be effective, communicating the importance of what they are doing, and reinforcing the priority of prayer. Also have handouts and written expectations of what is involved. This helps answer volunteers' questions and helps hold them accountable. Training should be brief but comprehensive. Ideally, it should occur within one week after volunteers enlist.
4. *Testimonies.* Schedule testimonies in the service from two to four weeks after the launch to report what has happened in participants' lives.

## Step 5: Develop a Renewal Strategy

**THE PASTOR AND LAYPERSON'S GOAL: TO KEEP THE SERVICE TO GOD FRESH**

As I have talked with prayer coordinators, I have heard a repeating theme: it is easier to start a prayer ministry than to maintain one. After launching a prayer ministry, people may begin to drop out after a few months. Reasons vary for the dropout rate, and some are beyond your control. However, one you can control is renewal. Renewal must be done on both short- and long-term bases. On a short-term basis, give attention to the five elements of leadership, communication, feedback, reinforcement, and celebration, which are described below. On a long-term basis, give attention to all seven elements that follow.

## Recruit Leaders

Although all ministries thrive on good leadership, it is especially true of prayer ministries because of their difficulty. Prayer warriors often pray alone and don't receive as much human interaction, encouragement, or accountability as workers in other ministries. I recommend that you pair same-gender and husband-wife teams whenever possible. Satan aggressively opposes prayer ministries. Prayer requires a lot of self-discipline. Concrete results are not always obvious; prayer ministry doesn't receive many pats on the back. Prayer ministry requires a high degree of *intentional* attention to keep it vibrant.

Having a prayer leader or the equivalent for every 8 to 12 persons proves to be a good ratio to keep participants encouraged and focused. For example, most intercessory prayer-room ministries have care leaders who call, write letters, or meet with their intercessors. The same pattern holds true in other prayer ministries, such as those who pray for Sunday-morning services or who are the pastor's prayer partners. Make sure someone is always in charge of keeping the others encouraged.

## Communicate

Communicate to the church and the intercessors what God is doing. Two things fuel encouragement: answered prayer and fresh information. People become discouraged when they pray and have no way to find out whether God is answering their prayers. It is imperative that you find ways to keep your intercessors informed about what God did when they prayed. Any number of ways may work—mailing letters, having a testimony time in church, posting answers to prayer on a bulletin board, starting the phone chain when God moves, for example.

Fresh information is also vital. Suppose your prayer list has several requests similar to this:

> Please pray for my father. He will have open-heart surgery August 13, and he is lost.

If it's now October, you can be sure that you will have many discouraged intercessors. Suppose that the prayer requests have been updated with information such as:

> Called his daughter August 19. She said the doctors almost lost him on the operating table, but miraculously, they were able to pull him through. He recognizes this as God's goodness to him, and he has become open to spiritual things. Keep praying!

Because of the update, both the church and the intercessors will be encouraged and will know how to continue praying.

## Gather Feedback

If no avenue exists for the congregation and intercessors to communicate with you, then you have no way of gauging their passion or God's work in their lives. Finding ways to gather feedback is absolutely indispensable in renewal. In fact, you can save a lot of rebuilding efforts if you know when the first signs of a waning passion occur.

Many ministries provide avenues of feedback when they launch a particular program but fail to keep the feedback ongoing. Continual feedback requires more energy short-term but pays great dividends long-term by keeping people motivated and by preventing problems.

## Reinforce the Importance of Prayer

Here are two ways to do this.

*Congregational visibility.* By maintaining congregational awareness, you will communicate the vital nature of the prayer ministry, you will encourage people to use and be involved in the prayer ministry, and you will encourage intercessors. Periodically highlight the importance of prayer and the ministry to the congregation through the various promotional strategies mentioned on page 22.

*Public affirmation.* When you catch somebody doing something right, praise the person verbally, by letter, or by phone. Do this both privately and publicly. This encouragement will motivate the person and others watching to understand the truth and do it.

## Celebrate

God established in the life cycle of the Jewish people a time for celebration. Studies have shown that celebration in attitude and on official occasions is an indispensable element in vibrant ministries. Therefore, your prayer ministry needs to have set times to celebrate what God is doing. Also, if the Lord does something exceptional, the response should be to immediately hold a meeting or service to celebrate.

Building an attitude of celebration by constantly giving thanks to God and praising Him will have a tremendous impact on your prayer ministry. This attitude will reinforce expectations of who God is and what He does when His people pray. Celebrating God's greatness also reminds people that God expects them to be like the One they celebrate.

## Plan Annually

When launching a prayer ministry, let your leaders know on the front end that you will have a yearly time of planning. This annual meeting provides several benefits.

*A time to regroup.* Resting and refocusing put priorities in their proper perspective. Also, energy is renewed to begin again.

*An opportunity to remove clutter.* All ministries develop excessive activities over time. Although the activities are usually good, they create two problems. First, they may cause us to substitute the good for the best. Second, an excessive number of activities leads to busywork, and busywork undercuts passion. To renew your ministry, periodically eliminate good but overburdening activities. Make sure your prayer programs qualify as the best instead of the good.

*A time to evaluate the effectiveness and direction of the ministry.* Carefully examine the evidence of God's blessings on your work. Consider these questions.

- To what degree are our people becoming a praying people?
- Are we affecting the whole church or just segments?
- What has gone well? Why?
- What has gone badly? Why?
- Where is God leading? What adjustments do we need to make?
- What is our balance between inward and outward praying?

*An opportunity to develop a long-range strategy.* To build a praying people, a church must comprehensively plan to utilize all of its resources to influence members in all possible areas. Annual planning provides an objective look at God's work and direction in the church.

## Make Budgeting a Priority

Typically, most people don't think of prayer as requiring a budget. The mentality "Well, how much does it cost to pray?" pervades the minds of many churches. Anything done well, however, requires resources to bring it about. The prayer ministry is no exception. Dollars should be set aside for promotion, printing, supplies, and other costs.

The appendix provides blank and sample budget sheets to assist you in determining your annual prayer-ministry budget.

# Step 6: Develop a Long-Range Strategy

> THE PASTOR AND LAYPERSON'S GOAL: TO CREATE STRATEGIES FOR INTERNAL AND EXTERNAL IMPACT

After the first prayer-ministry program is established and is functioning well, the prayer team can turn its attention to comprehensively incorporating prayer into the whole church. The following two elements and substeps create a dynamic long-range strategy.

## Create an Internal Strategy for Developing a Praying Church

Part of a church's long-range prayer strategy is to encourage growth by increasing spiritual depth and maximizing participation.

*Develop leaders.* In Scripture God chose to appoint leaders to shepherd His people and mobilize them to advance the Kingdom. Because this is a biblical pattern, you must seek to expand your leadership base if you hope to increase the depth and extent of prayer in your church.

You must have a strategy not only for identifying leaders but especially for developing their character. In the Bible whenever God selected a leader, He always sought to develop his character. The degree of the leader's character development was the degree of impact God granted through that life. This explains why Abraham, Joseph, David, and Paul had waiting times of years before they received their greatest assignments. God was developing their character to match their assignments. Virtues such as faith, integrity, humility, faithfulness, and love are much more important to God than skills and techniques are. Therefore, God's future activity will not surpass the character of the leaders.

*Disciple members.* The prayer team should pray for and seek ways to involve all church members in prayer training. Your goal should be to help them develop their relationship with God one-to-one and to learn to seek God's interests through prayer. I know of no better resources to do this than *Disciple's Prayer Life* and *In God's Presence* (see the resource list beginning on p. 109 in chap. 7). These courses allow for individual study and small-group interaction, creating the best-case scenario for learning, practice, and support.

In developing your discipleship strategy, also consider these questions.

- How do I help motivate members? People do not respond unless first motivated. Think of ways to help people understand the biblical commandments to pray and ways God will enrich their lives through a deep prayer life.
- How do we assimilate new converts and members? Often, new members are not aware of discipleship opportunities. How will you get the word to them?
- What level of commitment can you expect from members? Different believers are at different stages in their walks with God. Their willingness to commit to prayer will vary.

*Target networks of relationships.* Among churches that have started traditional prayer ministries, most have discovered that a relatively small percentage of the congregation participates in it, usually around 10 percent. Why? Although it cannot be directly proved from Scripture, I believe that just as all Christians have the assignment of evangelism though not all are evangelists, all Christians have the assignment of praying though not all are prayer warriors. I recommend acknowledging the reality that most church members will not become involved in an intensively focused, high-commitment prayer program. However, that does not mean the responsibility of leading the church to pray ends there. Instead, a different strategy ought to be developed for mobilizing all of the church body to pray.

For whom do you pray most? Your friend or a missionary you heard about overseas but don't know personally? Any prayer strategy for the entire church must be built on this truth: we pray most for those we know best. To mobilize the whole church to pray, organize around existing relationships. These relationships are found in choir, Sunday School, discipleship groups, or wherever ongoing groups exist. Because these persons know one another, they will naturally pray for one another.

This principle may explain why so few people commit to the traditional intercessory prayer-room ministry. The structure takes people out of the bases of relationships they already have and drops them in an environment in which they don't have a network of support. This does not mean the intercessory prayer room is not a valid ministry but that it will involve only a certain segment of the congregation. Usually, only prayer warriors will volunteer for or ultimately stick with this type of ministry.

So take advantage of ongoing relationships in the church by mobilizing existing groups to pray. Designate a prayer leader in each group.

*Make prayer follow purpose.* In Scripture whenever God's people prayed corporately and God did mighty things, they always had a singleness of purpose. When Pentecost came, the believers were in the upper room awaiting the Holy Spirit. When the angel freed Peter from prison, all were asking God for that one thing. When God's presence filled the temple, the whole nation was gathered before God for that single purpose.

When you organize any group to pray, it must have a purpose. For example, if you want to create a prayer network in a Sunday School class, members must agree to seek God for the same purpose, or prayer will become perfunctory and dry. Because people by nature tend to gravitate to their own world, the prayer leader must exercise intentional effort to maintain the focus. Lead the whole class to agree on the one thing they want God to do and display it visibly in the classroom. Thus, it becomes a visual reminder of your purpose.

Please do not interpret this section to mean that requests should not be taken for personal concerns.

In fact, if that element is missing, prayer dies as well; however, that is usually not the problem in most groups. Most err by losing a God-centered purpose. Your purpose could be a number of things, but typically, some type of outreach is a good place to begin.

*Have a base from which to operate.* Most prayer ministries that function well start with one ministry and then add others. For example, the intercessory prayer room functions as the centerpiece of many prayer ministries. For others the base may be the midweek prayer meeting or home meetings. Whatever the base, it should be a springboard to help promote the awareness of the need to pray, a place where your goals for the congregation are being met, and a platform from which new ministries can be launched.

## Create an External Strategy for Your Church to Serve God Through Prayer

Healthy praying is like breathing. You must inhale and exhale to survive. Doing only one or the other is lethal. So it is with prayer. An inward or outward focus alone harms a relationship with God. There must be balance. When a church errs in one direction, it usually gravitates toward an inward focus. The best cures are to constantly remind people of their intercessory roles as priests and to guide them in opportunities to intercede. Following are types of prayer ministries God has used to encourage deliberate intercession.

*Maximize your midweek prayer service.* Perhaps the greatest opportunity to remind the church body as a whole of its intercessory role as priests can best be done during the churchwide midweek prayer service. Any prayer strategy will include ways to revitalize and strengthen the midweek prayer meeting. Chapter 4 deals extensively with this subject, but I want to briefly mention two characteristics from history that caused these meetings to be powerful.

*Laity-driven.* A survey of Christian history in the 19th century reveals unprecedented gains in our nation. Not surprisingly, the prominence of prayer meetings coincided with this era, eventually resulting in the first regular weekly prayer meetings on a broad scale. Two major differences separated the prayer meetings of that era from ours. First, they were laity-driven. Often, pastors were either in short supply, forcing lay people to be responsible for their own prayer meetings, or the structure of the meeting generated a high level of participation. Toward the latter decades, though, a most detrimental development occurred that minimized the laity's involvement. Recognizing prayer's importance and wishing to conduct the meetings in the most beneficial manner, churches increasingly assumed that only the most "qualified" member should conduct the prayer meeting, so pastors took over. Although the intention may have been good, this move began diminishing churchwide participation. Over time the result was a weakened interest in prayer, the things of God, and the desire to be involved. Eventually, the pastor-dominated prayer service degenerated into a sermon or Bible study with token attention given to prayer. As a result, the people increasingly lost their savor as salt and light in society.

*Evangelistic.* Second, almost all special prayer meetings for the first 65 years of the 19th century had the spread of the gospel and/or missions as their primary emphasis. After the Civil War, however, this element began losing prominence. Interestingly, the loss of laity-driven meetings and the decreased emphasis on the spread of the gospel and/or missions occurred almost simultaneously. Eventually, the prayer meetings ceased to be outwardly focused and became more inwardly focused.

The legacy of these two developments bequeathed us a modern-day inheritance of services called prayer meetings, which in reality are mainly teaching or preaching sessions. When prayer is held, audience participation is weak, and the requests for the sick (inward focus) dominate, minimizing or excluding prayers for changing the world around us (outward focus). Structure this service to be laity-driven and outwardly focused.

*Make missions and evangelism a priority.* The importance of praying for missions cannot be overstated. After reading the Bible for years, I can find only one thing the Father commanded the Son to pray for:

" 'Ask of Me, and I will surely
    give the nations as Thine inheritance.
And the very ends of the earth
    as Thy possession' " (Ps. 2:8, NASB).

The Father's heart is to give the whole earth to His

Son. Any prayer strategy that wants to be close to God's heart must make this priority central. Ways to do this vary from prayer groups to the intercessory prayer room to churchwide prayer meetings. On pages 101 and 105 you will find networks, projects, and resources that can help your church pray for missionaries and unreached people groups.

Evangelism is being on mission with God locally. Churches that highlight the importance of praying for lost people see God work in mighty ways. Praying for missions and evangelism ought to be an integral part of all prayer meetings and the subject of specific, focused prayer meetings. Guidance for conducting evangelistic prayer meetings is provided on pages 50–52, and other ideas for evangelistic praying can be found in chapter 5.

*Provide opportunities for intercession.* Following are two types of highly focused intercessory prayer ministries God has used to encourage deliberate intercession. Although you are not limited to these methods, they are presented as popular choices.

*Intercessory prayer room.* Chapter 3 deals extensively with developing an intercessory prayer room. It is a proven way members can intentionally lift up others to God.

*Purpose groups.* Many people in the church will have a particular area they feel strongly about. As prayer leaders, you may want to harness that passion by forming prayer groups with specific callings. Examples are Moms in Touch (concerned mothers who pray for their schools), Adopt-a-Cop (praying for policemen), and Lighthouses of Prayer (family prayer groups that target praying for their lost friends, coworkers, or neighbors). These types of prayer groups, several of which are described in chapter 5, afford ways people can pray with an outward focus.

*Support other church ministries.* Another function of any prayer ministry is to support the church's ministries. God's power in Sunday School, worship services, Vacation Bible School, and other ministries must be sought. A church that is successful in these arenas must pray that God will prosper their work. There are multiple ways to accomplish this. If you have an intercessory prayer room, you will certainly want to utilize it, but perhaps an indispensable strategy is to organize prayer groups among those involved in the ministries themselves.

*Develop appropriate strategies for events.* Special events pepper the church calendar, such as seminars, Christmas programs, high-attendance Sundays, and revivals. Strategies need to be developed to support them. Various churches have responded by holding all-night prayer meetings in the sanctuary, organizing members into a continuous chain of prayer the week before an event, creating prayer magnets for the refrigerator or bumper stickers for the car, or holding cottage prayer meetings through the Sunday School network. The options are limited only by your creativity.

Your prayer ministry will grow over time. You can add ministries as the interest and number of prayer warriors increase. God may not lead you to do every one of these ideas, but strive for the long-range goal of comprehensively influencing the whole church.

## Becoming a House of Prayer

Jesus best described God's expectation of His church when He quoted Isaiah 56:7:

"My house will be called
a house of prayer for all nations" (NIV).

In the Old Testament God's house, or temple, was built of stone, but in the New Testament it was built of His people (see Eph. 2:19-22). The defining characteristic of that new house is that God's very presence would dwell among His people in a love relationship through prayer. No record exists in Scripture of another way God prefers to relate to His people.

Having a praying people is not just a good idea. It is the foundation from which everything else springs. God does not want our service and activity apart from a relationship with Him, and in fact, He will not accept them without it.

I pray that this chapter has contributed in some way to your working with God to till the hearts of your people so that you may please Him in every respect. May your church grow mightier and mightier in the Lord, and may you obtain the testimony of " ' "Well done, good and faithful servant!" ' " (Matt. 25:21, NIV).

# CHAPTER 3

# *The* INTERCESSORY PRAYER ROOM

## ELAINE HELMS

The heartbeat of many prayer ministries is the intercessory prayer room. Although many people think of a prayer room as a small, chapel-like room that has been created for individuals to visit and pray in a quiet, worshipful atmosphere, the prayer room we will discuss in this chapter is a working room, a place where much information is filed for many different people to retrieve easily for use in intercession. This locked room keeps prayer requests confidential, available only to trained, scheduled intercessors.

The purpose of an intercessory-prayer-room ministry is to pray comprehensively for God's concerns as well as for the concerns of church members and others. The ministry collects, organizes, and prays for various types of requests, some of which are missions, salvation, health, finances, and others the church wishes to focus on. If possible, the intercessory-prayer-room ministry should also seek to maintain continuous prayer before God by enlisting intercessors to pray in one-hour time slots. A church's size determines how many hours in the day are filled, but the constancy of prayer is important because the prayers of saints are a pleasing fragrance to God (see Rev. 8:3-4).

Planning is needed for an intercessory prayer room

to function effectively. In this chapter we will discuss how to design and equip the room; how to create a system; how to promote the intercessory-prayer-room ministry; how to enlist intercessors; and how to maintain the room for a successful, thriving ministry.

## Organizing an Intercessory-Prayer-Room Ministry

### Respond to God

The best way to begin an intercessory-prayer-room ministry is to seek God's plan for your church. Ideally, the pastor should recognize the necessity of prayer and desire that the church be a house of prayer as Jesus directed. Involving the pastor as much as possible is vital, because he, more than anyone else, has the platform to inform people on the importance of prayer. If you and the pastor sense that an intercessory prayer room is the right way to express this need, then you are ready for the next step.

### Select a Coordinator

Begin the organizational process by selecting an intercessory-prayer-room coordinator. Make sure this person has integrity before God and the church's respect, because the coordinator will play the pivotal role in establishing and maintaining the intercessory prayer room. This person's leadership and supervision, to a great degree, will determine the ministry's success.

The intercessory-prayer-room coordinator's major responsibilities include the following.

---

**RESPONSIBILITIES OF AN INTERCESSORY-PRAYER-ROOM COORDINATOR**

- Work closely with the pastor and/or staff to launch the intercessory-prayer-room ministry.
- Select, with the pastor's approval, an intercessory-prayer-room committee.
- Oversee the intercessory-prayer-room committee and the design and implementation of the ministry, including location, furnishings, processes, and forms.
- Plan and develop a budget.
- Oversee promotion and congregational awareness.
- Enlist and train intercessors.
- Complete and submit a weekly accountability report to the appropriate staff member.
- Develop a strategy for maintaining and renewing the ministry.
- Cooperate with other program personnel to ensure that the ministry supports all church ministries and activities.
- Oversee the planning of an annual appreciation banquet to honor intercessors and to reinforce the importance of the ministry.

---

### Form a Committee

Next, an intercessory-prayer-room committee should be formed to help execute the duties required to establish and maintain the intercessory-prayer-room ministry. The committee should include representatives from all areas of church life, for example, men, women, singles, seniors, youth, and married. Also include key program areas, such as music, missions, and education. The size of the committee will be determined by the needs and complexity of your intercessory-prayer-room ministry. As few as two or three members are acceptable, and most committees should not exceed eight.

When you recruit committee members, clearly define their roles and responsibilities. Following are an intercessory-prayer-room committee member's duties.

---

**RESPONSIBILITIES OF AN INTERCESSORY-PRAYER-ROOM COMMITTEE**

- Participate in the ministry as an intercessor.
- Work with the coordinator to design and implement the ministry, including location, furnishings, processes, and forms.
- Work with the coordinator to promote the ministry.
- Work with the coordinator to develop and implement ways to renew the ministry.
- Help with the annual appreciation banquet.
- Execute other duties as needed.

---

After the intercessory-prayer-room coordinator and committee have been selected, they are ready to begin planning and implementing the intercessory-prayer-room ministry. The chart on page 30 illustrates the major steps involved, the persons who are responsible, and a rough time line for completing the planning steps.

## Designing and Equipping the Intercessory Prayer Room

### Find a Suitable Location

If the intercessory prayer room is part of a new building, plans can be made for best using the space and for locating the room in a quiet part of the building. Because this is not usually the case, the room will probably be a converted space in existing facilities. Try to locate the intercessory prayer room away from areas used for noisy activities. Consider lighting and heat ducts if walls are created or moved. Take note of any rewiring or plumbing that will need to be done. Make sure the room has a secured combination or keypad lock on the door because of the confidential nature of the ministry. The room's size may vary, but it needs to be large enough to hold a desk or a large table, two chairs, a bookcase, and a storage closet or cabinet. Optional but important features are an altar and a rest room. Having an outside entrance is beneficial for the security of the

| ESTABLISHING AN INTERCESSORY-PRAYER-ROOM MINISTRY | | |
|---|---|---|
| Action | Assigned To | Completion Date Before Launch |
| ❑  1. Realize need for intercessory-prayer-room ministry. | Pastor, staff, and laypersons | 4–6 months |
| ❑  2. Select intercessory-prayer-room coordinator and committee. | Pastor and/or coordinator | 3–4 months |
| ❑  3. Identify intercessory-prayer-room location and needed furnishings. | Coordinator and committee | 2–3 months |
| ❑  4. Create intercessory-prayer-room process. | Coordinator and committee | 2–3 months |
| ❑  5. Propose intercessory-prayer-room ministry to church. | Pastor and coordinator | 6–8 weeks |
| ❑  6. Secure prayer-line telephone number. | Coordinator and committee | 6 weeks |
| ❑  7. Order supplies and print forms. | Coordinator and committee | 5–6 weeks |
| ❑  8. Promote intercessory prayer room and enlist intercessors. | Coordinator and committee | 2–5 weeks |
| ❑  9. Hold open house. | Coordinator and committee | 2 weeks |
| ❑ 10. Have Commitment Sunday. | Coordinator and committee | 2 weeks |
| ❑ 11. Make assignments and train intercessors. | Coordinator and committee | 1 week |
| ❑ 12. Launch ministry. | Intercessors | |

rest of the building, as well as for intercessors' ease of access.

**Provide Furnishings**

If your church has any decorators, enlist several to plan, design, and furnish the intercessory prayer room. Or you could hire a decorator to make the most of your funds and space. Before enlisting a decorator's help, either volunteer or hired, ask for samples of the person's work, locations, or photographs so that you can determine which ones best suit your church's needs. The intercessory prayer room needs to be functional, as well as attractive and comfortable.

Provide a desk or a table to hold supplies, forms, and requests for intercessors to use conveniently. One design has a shelf at the back that is connected to an angled surface against which intercessors can prop notebooks and forms. Many people will use the desk, so choose one that is best for your situation and budget.

The main desk chair should be neither too comfortable nor too straight, neither too big nor too small. Look for a business desk chair with adequate back support. A swivel base will help intercessors reach adjacent shelves and turn to read bulletin boards without getting up. Because it will be used frequently, choose the best-quality chair you can

afford. The second chair, for times when couples come together, can be a side chair that does not swivel. Because it will be used less frequently, it does not have to be of high quality.

Focus a desk lamp's lighting where intercessors write prayergrams or read. Offer a choice of strong, bright lighting and soft, dim lighting to accommodate intercessors' preferences. Plan overhead or spot lighting to illuminate bulletin and dry-erase boards.

Bulletin boards will be needed to display urgent prayer requests, current church activities, mission trips, answered prayers, and thank-you notes. Having separate boards for urgent requests and answered prayer is suggested to avoid confusion. If space is limited, combine churchwide requests and urgent ones. A dry-erase board is also a valuable tool to display three names at a time, in alphabetical order, from the salvation requests you will accumulate.

Storage is a major consideration in a prayer room. Place a bookcase or shelves adjacent to the desk to keep needed resources close at hand. A separate shelf could be installed on the wall for additional storage. A closet with shelves is good for storing forms and other supplies out of sight. As the ministry grows, more space will be needed for keeping things in order.

Use the checklists on page 31 to identify items you want to include in your intercessory prayer room.

| INTERCESSORY-PRAYER-ROOM FURNISHINGS |
| --- |
| ❏ Desk, built-in or free-standing |
| ❏ Two chairs |
| ❏ Bookcase |
| ❏ Altar, built-in or free-standing |
| ❏ Desk lamp and overhead lighting |
| ❏ Bulletin boards |
| ❏ Dry-erase board |
| ❏ Closet or storage space |
| ❏ Rest room, if possible |
| ❏ Coatrack or coat closet |
| ❏ Trash can |
| ❏ Outside door with peephole if no adjacent window |
| ❏ Security light outside |
| ❏ Window treatments |
| ❏ Mailbox—desktop, hanging, or on a stand |
| ❏ Telephone with voicemail or answering machine |
| ❏ Computer |
| ❏ Decorative accessories, mirror, stained glass |
| ❏ Candy dish for individually wrapped mints |

| INTERCESSORY-PRAYER-ROOM RESOURCES AND SUPPLIES |
| --- |
| ❏ Bible and concordance |
| ❏ Bible-promise books |
| ❏ Hymnal |
| ❏ Prayer-room handbook |
| ❏ Telephone books and ZIP-code directory |
| ❏ Dictionary and medical dictionary |
| ❏ Pens and pencils |
| ❏ Pushpins for bulletin boards |
| ❏ Paper clips |
| ❏ Tape in dispenser |
| ❏ Scissors |
| ❏ Holder(s) for supplies on desk |
| ❏ Tissues |
| ❏ Notepads |
| ❏ Notebooks to hold various forms |
| ❏ Plastic covers for forms |
| ❏ Rotary files or card-file boxes |
| ❏ Calendar |
| ❏ Clock |

### Establish a Budget

As you research and price items and any remodeling work needed for your intercessory prayer room, you will get an idea of the size budget you will need. Also consider the cost of maintaining the intercessory prayer room and the total intercessory-prayer-room ministry, including such items as promotion, printing, and the annual prayer banquet. Find out whether the church budget will cover lights, heating and cooling, water, telephone installation and service, postage, and office supplies or whether those expenses must be included in the intercessory prayer room's budget. If prayer events for intercessors will be offered, add those cost estimates as well. Budgeting may seem overwhelming at first, but counting the cost is a biblical principle: " 'Which one of you, when he wants to build a tower, does not first sit down and calculate the cost, to see if he has enough to complete it?' " (Luke 14:28, NASB).

Something interesting happened to one church group that was starting an intercessory prayer room. The committee went to a furniture store to price the necessary items to set up a room. When the owner heard what they were doing, he donated the desk, two chairs, and a lamp. Always pray about what you need to start your intercessory-prayer-room ministry. God will provide for what He calls you to do and will often use other people to answer prayers for His kingdom work.

## Creating a System

A commitment to pray for each prayer request received is a core component of an intercessory-prayer-room ministry. To carry out this commitment, establish a system and set policies for handling requests and for conducting follow-up. Also prepare printed materials needed by intercessors, including forms and instructional booklets. It is often helpful to use different colors for different forms, especially request cards. A checklist of these materials is provided on page 32. Samples of the forms are provided in the appendix, beginning on page 112. Adapt them to meet your church's needs.

### Establish a Process

Before the intercessory prayer room is opened and

## INTERCESSORY-PRAYER-ROOM FORMS AND TOOLS

❏ *Care leader's monthly report.* Record each intercessor's attendance for follow-up.

❏ *Church-staff prayer request.* This form is used to receive personal and ministry requests from the church staff.

❏ *Commitment card.* This card is used to register intercessors when the ministry begins.

❏ *Coordinator's weekly report.* This is an accountability record of attendance, calls, answered prayers, mailings, and other intercessory prayer-room activities.

❏ *Enrollment sheet.* This sheet is used to enroll intercessors and to record the hours they have chosen to pray.

❏ *Handbook.* This is a necessary tool for training intercessors and for reference as intercessors serve. It can contain classic quotes on prayer to inspire them, as well as an explanation of the intercessory-prayer-room ministry and expectations for intercessors. It might also include an encouraging note from the pastor and a welcome note from the intercessory-prayer-room coordinator or committee.

❏ *Prayergram.* This one-piece card, which folds to be addressed, is for writing encouraging notes from the intercessory prayer room.

❏ *Prayer-request card.* This one-sided card is used to receive prayer requests from outside the intercessory prayer room.

❏ *Promotional card.* This piece promotes the intercessory-prayer-room ministry.

❏ *Referral or helps notebook.* This notebook includes names, addresses, and phone numbers for local hospitals, crisis hot lines, Christian counselors, shelters, the benevolent screening service you use for nonmembers who need help, and other needed data. Protect pages in clear plastic to prolong their life.

❏ *Sign-in sheet.* This daily or weekly sheet reveals which intercessors are serving.

❏ *Telephone-request card.* This card is used to record requests called in.

❏ *Update postcard.* This preprinted card with a caring message requests prayer-request updates.

❏ *Urgent-request card.* Identical to the telephone-request card, it is printed on brightly colored card stock and is placed on the urgent board.

intercessors are enlisted, answer the question, What will we pray about? Plan a process for collecting, organizing, updating, and discontinuing prayer requests. An easy-to-use process will ensure that requests are handled efficiently and that intercessors are satisfied. A suggested process is depicted on page 33. Let's walk through each step one by one.

### Collect Prayer Requests

Prayer requests will come from several sources, including the pew, prayer-request boxes, telephone, prayer guides, mail, and others. Several of these sources will require administrative effort. For example, you must make sure you have a way to collect prayer-request cards placed in offering plates or in prayer-request boxes and to take them to the intercessory prayer room. A prescribed process for collecting all prayer-request cards demonstrates your commitment to prayer and shows concern for others.

### Organize Prayer Requests

As the number of prayer requests increases, you will need to organize them in such a way that intercessors can focus their prayer efforts. You can organize requests in any number of ways, from file boxes to notebooks. Someone will need to be responsible for filing the requests, perhaps the first intercessor of the day or the intercessory-prayer-room coordinator. Many churches have found it helpful to first place request cards in a "Current" box to ensure that the newest requests are prayed for first. After two weeks they are filed according to categories.

Decide on the number of categories you want to introduce in the beginning. Keep it simple and allow the ministry to grow. You may wish to start with three or four categories and increase as other types of requests come in. Consider the categories in the box on page 34.

# THE INTERCESSORY-PRAYER-ROOM PROCESS

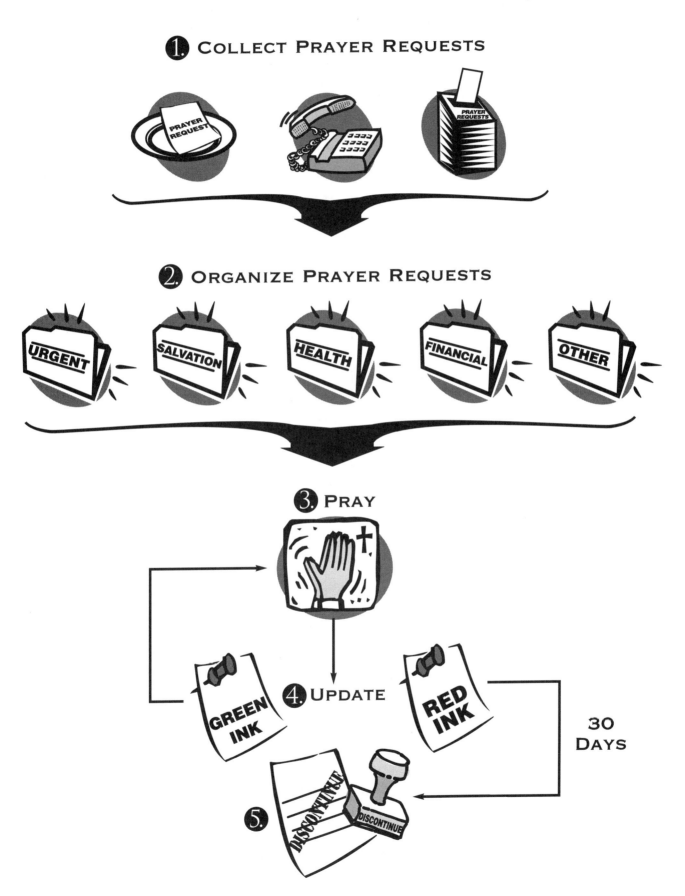

**1. COLLECT PRAYER REQUESTS**

**2. ORGANIZE PRAYER REQUESTS**

URGENT SALVATION HEALTH FINANCIAL OTHER

**3. PRAY**

**4. UPDATE**

GREEN INK RED INK

**5.** DISCONTINUE

30 DAYS

## CATEGORIES FOR INTERCESSION

- *Church leaders.* These requests come from the pastor, other church staff, deacons, teachers, and committee chairpersons.
- *Church members.* Use a directory or printout that can be highlighted or initialed to show who has been prayed for and to mark the place to start praying.
- *Elected national, state, and local officials.* Focus on a few needs rather than attempt to pray for too many.
- *Missionaries.* Use a prayer calendar to manage prayers for missionaries supported by the church and/or denomination.
- *Requests from prayer-request cards.* These cards, representing requests made outside the intercessory prayer room, are placed in the offering plate, dropped in a prayer-request box, or brought by the prayer room.
- *Requests from telephone-request cards.* These requests are taken and recorded by intercessors who receive calls in the intercessory prayer room.
- *Urgent requests on bulletin boards.* These requests center on situations like accidents and surgery, which are posted in the intercessory prayer room.

As prayer requests enter the intercessory prayer room, categorize them according to the subject areas selected. As the number of requests grows, additional categories of prayer-request cards may become necessary. Additional topics for prayer requests may include healing, salvation, family needs, churches and other ministries, job needs, and encouragement.

### Update Prayer Requests

One of the most important tasks in operating an intercessory prayer room is keeping the prayer requests updated and current. Decide in advance how intercessors will follow up on requests to keep them current and to learn how God has answered them. The more requests you receive, the more people you may need to help update them. Always encourage callers to call back with updates. Place notices in the church newsletter or order of worship inviting people to share prayer requests and to encourage them to give updates or share answers to prayers. This initiative communicates that you care about them.

One intercessor suggested using a colored-pen system for prayer requests. The original request is written in blue or black ink. Then updates are written in green ink. Just as a green traffic light tells you to keep driving, green ink tells you to keep praying! When the prayer is answered, write the answer and praise in red ink, which corresponds to a red traffic light. When you use color coding, the answered-prayer board is colorful and exciting. Color coding also makes it easier to find and pray for current information.

### Discontinue Prayer Requests

Some requests will need to be prayed for longer than others. Decide how long you will pray for requests and how much effort will be made to update them. If you have no way to follow up, it will be necessary to discontinue praying after a set period of time. Some churches print this disclaimer on their prayer-request cards: "We will pray for your request for 30 days. If you have additional or changed information or would like continued prayer beyond that time, please call the prayer line." Such a statement communicates that persons requesting prayer are responsible for requesting continued prayer beyond the set time.

## Promoting and Enlisting

### Promote in the Church

Before the opening day of the intercessory prayer room, it is important to inspire the congregation and promote the benefits an intercessory prayer room offers. As the pastor preaches on prayer and announcements are made about the opening, church members' interest level will grow. The objective is to enlist people to serve in the intercessory prayer room, to use prayer-request cards, and to call the prayer line.

Two keys to a successful intercessory prayer room are people who commit to pray and people who share prayer requests. Although receiving requests may be easier than finding dedicated intercessors, do not lose heart. Only God through the Holy Spirit can truly call out the intercessors, and He wants them more than we do: Jesus "said to His disciples, 'The harvest is plentiful, but the workers are few. Therefore beseech the Lord of the harvest to send out workers into His harvest' " (Matt. 9:37-38, NASB).

An obvious, though sometimes overlooked, step in beginning an intercessory prayer room is prayer. From the research to the planning to the installation to the recruiting, stay close to the Father and act in His will, and He will direct your steps. I learned the hard way that if I stir a lot of excitement and cajole people to enroll to serve in the intercessory prayer room, they probably won't last; some never even show up. However, if the Holy Spirit calls the intercessors, they prove to be steadfast and faithful prayer warriors. Make sure the prayer committee prays to the Lord of the harvest throughout your planning stages.

For the congregation to make a decision about serving, they need exposure to basic information about the intercessory-prayer-room ministry. Use the following ideas to promote your intercessory prayer room.

- Ask the pastor to preach sermons on prayer leading up to a Commitment Sunday.
- Make announcements in Sunday School classes.
- Teach lessons on prayer in Sunday School classes to let God's Word speak clearly on prayer.
- Share testimonies about answered prayer in classes, worship services, or both.
- Place articles on prayer in the church newsletter.
- Print notices in the church newsletter or order of worship.
- Have children make posters in their Sunday School classes depicting their ideas about the intercessory prayer room.
- Mail letters from the pastor inviting all church members to become involved.
- Send enlarged samples of a prayergram to all members to let them know that they will continually be prayed for when the intercessory prayer room opens. Include a note inviting them to pray about serving as intercessors. Give the date, time, and place for intercessory-prayer-room training.
- When the intercessory prayer room is ready, hold an open house to generate interest. Serve refreshments and explain to church members the way your ministry will operate.
- Plan a commitment service to officially begin your intercessory prayer-room ministry. The pastor can invite all who are willing to serve to come forward for a prayer of commitment.

## Promote in the Community

If you will have a prayer-line telephone number, try to arrange for the last four digits to be 7729 so that your number will correspond to the letters P-R-A-Y. If that isn't possible, try another prayer term that can be easily communicated to and remembered by the community.

- Print the prayer-line number on church materials and in advertisements for services.
- Send letters for public-service announcements to local Christian radio stations.
- Print business cards with the prayer-line number for members to give to persons who need prayer. These could be left in such places as hotel lobbies, waiting rooms, hospitals, and funeral homes.
- Some billboard companies provide public-service announcements for a nominal fee to cover materials and installation.

## Training Intercessors

On Commitment Sunday have cards ready to distribute that remind members of the training time and that inform them of the requirements to be an intercessor. Here are the major commitments most intercessory-prayer-room ministries require of their intercessors.

### RESPONSIBILITIES OF AN INTERCESSOR

- Attend training.
- Be faithful to your assigned hours in the intercessory prayer room.
- Pray for the requests in the intercessory prayer room.
- Write prayergrams as needed.
- Pray with callers if your ministry has a prayer line.
- Keep confidential matters confidential.

During your training session teach intercessors the process that will be used in the intercessory-prayer-room ministry, presented earlier in this chapter. Also make sure intercessors know the whys of prayer and the intercessory prayer room. Emphasize intercessors' personal relationships with Jesus. Encourage them to grow and spend time in personal Bible study and prayer in addition to their appointed hours in the intercessory prayer room each week. More important than their ability is their availability to God. This is a spiritual ministry, and the Holy Spirit equips intercessors to pray effectively.

As your intercessory-prayer-room ministry becomes known, it is likely that seekers of the truth will call. It is important to place tracts and plans for sharing the gospel in a convenient place in the intercessory prayer room for intercessors to use. As a part of the training, encourage intercessors to be ready for opportunities to share the gospel: "Sanctify Christ as Lord in your hearts, always being ready to make a defense to everyone who asks you to give an account for the hope that is in you, yet with gentleness and reverence" (1 Pet. 3:15, NASB).

**Teach Intercessors How to Use Their Time**
At the beginning of an intercessory prayer-room ministry, many intercessors ask themselves, *How can I pray for an hour and not repeat myself?* After they begin to serve, though, they usually conclude, *An hour is not enough time!* Give intercessors enough to pray about without overwhelming them with cumbersome or impossible expectations. Pray over and fine-tune your plan for using the hour until the committee feels it is workable.

As you prepare to train intercessors before they serve in the intercessory prayer room, try to answer the question, How can we best use the time so that all prayer requests are continually prayed for in an orderly fashion? One plan for spending the hour is suggested in the box at the top of the next column.

**Share Effective Telephone Techniques**
Any plans an intercessor has made for the hour will quickly change when the telephone rings. Therefore, stress to intercessors the need to be flexible. Phone calls are opportunities for ministry to the hurting, lonely, and lost, and they should never be considered interruptions. Remind intercessors that God is in control and that they serve in the intercessory prayer room to be available to Him. Intercessors are on His agenda, and He will equip them through the Holy Spirit to handle whatever He allows to come their way. Sometimes it seems as though God orchestrates the timing of the call to match the caller's need with

| SAMPLE PLAN FOR INTERCESSION | |
|---|---|
| 5 minutes | Prepare your heart by praising God, confessing sin, and/or reading the Bible. |
| 10 minutes | Pray for urgent and churchwide requests on the bulletin boards and for the names on the salvation board. |
| 10 minutes | Pray for requests on current and long-term prayer-request cards in each category. |
| 10 minutes | Pray for members and write one or two prayergrams. |
| 10 minutes | Pray for church leaders and missionaries. |
| 10 minutes | Pray for elected officials. |
| 5 minutes | Praise God as you read the answered-prayer board and thank-you notes. |

the victories He has had in the intercessor's life.

*Taking telephone requests.* Most calls are brief, clear, and to the point. Callers usually have specific requests they want you to pray for. The following instructions apply to this kind of call.
1. Answer the phone with something like "God answers prayer! This is [give name of church]. May I help you?"
2. Listen to the caller and repeat any unclear information to get it correct as you take notes. Try to find out whether the caller and the subject of prayer are Christians.
3. Check for correct spelling and get complete addresses if a note of encouragement or a prayergram is appropriate.
4. Pray with all callers over the phone before hanging up.
5. Ask the caller to notify the intercessory prayer room of updates, changes, or answers to prayer.
6. Write on a telephone-request card the information other intercessors will need to be able to pray. Try to make the request clear and concise, leaving room for updates.
7. As you pray again for the request, write a note on a prayergram to the caller thanking him or her for the call. Encourage other intercessors to call and update the information.

8. If the address is available and it is appropriate, also write a note to the subject of prayer.

*Handling repeat calls.* After word spreads that compassionate persons answer the phone at this number, lonely persons may call often, and the prayer line becomes a friend giving hope. Intercessors should be kind and polite without staying on the phone too long. With preparation the intercessors can handle these potentially difficult calls with grace. Intercessors should follow these steps.

1. Listen.
2. Show interest and Christian love.
3. Turn the conversation to prayer even when the caller has no particular request.
4. Be kind but firm in explaining that after praying with the caller, intercessors must get back to praying.
5. Tell the regular callers that intercessors pray for them.
6. Tell these callers that they are welcome to call as needed, but intercessors cannot stay on the phone for a long time.

Although in their own strength intercessors are inadequate to answer correctly and bless callers, the Holy Spirit helps them respond appropriately when they are available and willing vessels for His work. Intercessors should ask for a fresh filling of the Holy Spirit before answering the phone: "In the same way the Spirit also helps our weakness; for we do not know how to pray as we should, but the Spirit Himself intercedes for us with groanings too deep for words; and He who searches the hearts knows what the mind of the Spirit is, because He intercedes for the saints according to the will of God" (Rom. 8: 26-27, NASB).

*Resisting the urge to give advice.* Giving advice to callers is not advisable. When intercessors answer the prayer-line phone, they represent the church. A disclaimer to the effect that intercessors are not counselors can be shared with callers. Intercessors serve by praying for and with people. They can point callers to Jesus and Scripture but should never try to solve deep problems or give marital, financial, business, or career advice; express opinions about consumer products; or offer advice on other sensitive issues for which the church could be held liable.

In the same way, prayergrams are uplifting, positive notes of encouragement. To ensure that all notes

sent on behalf of the church meet this criterion, have intercessors put their outgoing prayergrams in the prayer-room mailbox, unsealed and unstamped. The intercessory-prayer-room coordinator or a member of the intercessory-prayer-room committee should be responsible for reading and mailing the prayergrams on a regular schedule. Judgmental notes or notes with advice or wrong theology need to be withheld. An encouraging visit with the writer of the note might be in order at this point.

## Emphasize Confidentiality
Explain to intercessors the importance of keeping prayer requests confidential. Tremendous trust is given to those who serve. Intercessors will learn about marital problems, financial difficulties, rebellious children, and other sensitive issues that callers would not want others to know about. It is vital to the success of the ministry that intercessors be trustworthy: "Let a man regard us in this manner, as servants of Christ, and stewards of the mysteries of God. In this case, moreover, it is required of stewards that one be found trustworthy" (1 Cor. 4: 1-2, NASB).

## Maintaining and Enriching the Ministry

### Enlist Care Leaders
As participation in the intercessory prayer room grows, enlist care leaders to help keep up with the intercessors. One way to divide the load is to enlist one care leader for every 12 intercessors, such as from midnight Monday to 11:00 a.m. Tuesday. Care leaders check the attendance book to see whether their group is being consistent. When they notice an absence, they call the intercessor to check on the person and to offer encouragement. Good questions to ask include "Did you forget to sign in?" and "How is that hour working out?" Intercessors may need to change their scheduled times. The care leader can alert the intercessory-prayer-room coordinator to potential problems and areas of concern.

### Maintain a Pleasant Atmosphere
Keeping the room neat, clean, and well supplied is important to encourage intercessors' faithfulness. To prevent pest problems, eating and drinking in the

room should not be allowed. A dish of individually wrapped mints and a water cooler could be made available. Fasting is a valuable part of prayer, and one hour is a short time to go without food.

## Plan Regular Meetings

Intercessors need to occasionally get together, meet one another, and share good experiences. Topical teaching can be offered, such as how to pray for the salvation of the lost or for missionaries. Intercessors are encouraged by these opportunities to see the bigger picture and to have their questions answered. Their prayer in agreement for the ministry and churchwide requests is powerful.

## Report Answered Prayers

The answered-prayer board is a source of encouragement to intercessors who serve in the intercessory prayer room each week. When people submit requests for prayer and see how God answers those prayers, they become excited. They often write notes to share their excitement and appreciation for intercessors' prayers. Thank-you notes can be displayed on the bulletin board in addition to answered prayers. Hearing about the ways God is working motivates intercessors to keep praying.

## Listen to Suggestions

As intercessors serve, they will have suggestions for improving the ministry. Invite them to write their suggestions and to place them in the mailbox along with prayergrams to be mailed. Incorporate their ideas when feasible. Ask intercessors not to make changes to the system themselves without approval. Let intercessors know when their ideas cannot be implemented due to reasons beyond your control.

## Pray for Intercessors

Write intercessors' names on the wall calendar so that they are prayed for on their birthdays. You might want to supply birthday cards in the prayer room so that intercessors can also send cards to one another. The prayer-room coordinator and/or the care leader should send cards to all intercessors on their birthdays.

## Eliminate Guilt

The commitment to serve in the intercessory prayer room should last one year. The enlistment of intercessors should be a special emphasis each year. Having a definite beginning and ending for service helps the ministry stay fresh. This also makes it easier for an intercessor who is called to another ministry for a season to leave the intercessory-prayer-room ministry on good terms. When departures are guilt-free, intercessors often return to the ministry after a year or two. A welcoming, noncondemning attitude toward those who do not serve augments the ministry's appeal and encourages church members to respond favorably to the ministry.

## Expanding the Ministry

### Promote Congregational Awareness

Keep the congregation aware of the intercessory prayer room. Place a bulletin board in a heavily traveled hallway or large gathering place in the church building. Thank-you notes for prayers and notes of encouragement can help open members' eyes to the ministry's impact in the community as well as in the church family.

### Feature Intercessors' Testimonies

Intercessors' written or verbal testimonies about why they serve in the intercessory prayer room can encourage others to participate in the ministry. Feature intercessors' testimonies in conjunction with an annual enlistment of intercessors.

### Encourage Class Involvement

Involve Sunday School classes or discipleship groups in the intercessory-prayer-room ministry by inviting them to commit to an hour assigned to members of the class or group. The commitment level is much less than for regular intercessors. This way someone can try the intercessory prayer room, knowing that it is only for one time or once a quarter. Many full-time intercessors start this way.

Classes or other groups like deacons, choir, church staff, or weekday Bible-study participants can also help cover difficult hours such as weekends. Even if intercessors serve only one time, they need to be trained. Exposure to the ministry helps the church body recognize the need for and importance of the intercessory prayer room.

### Hold a Churchwide Banquet

A churchwide prayer banquet can be an inspiring and motivational way to expose members to the ministry. By hearing testimonies of intercessors who have been serving or people who have benefited from intercessors' prayers, attendees grasp the significance of the ministry. Consider inviting a well-known speaker or a prayer warrior to speak from personal experience. An important feature of a prayer banquet is to recognize intercessors who have served in the intercessory prayer room. Music and good food add to the festive spirit, but the best part of such a gathering is praying around the tables in a directed way, focusing on churchwide requests rather than illnesses or personal requests. The senior pastor, the coordinator, or the invited speaker could lead the prayer time. When intercessors come together for corporate prayer, they leave encouraged about the ministry.

## Watch What God Does Through Intercessory Prayer

If God is calling your church to have an intercessory-prayer-room ministry, obey His call, stay close to Him, and watch what He will do. Enlist an intercessory-prayer-room committee to share the responsibility. With everyone using their spiritual gifts, the myriad details will pale in light of the joy and fulfillment that result from participating in a vital, growing intercessory-prayer-room ministry.

# CHAPTER 4

# KEYS *To* DYNAMIC PRAYER MEETINGS

## GREG FRIZZELL

In spite of America's staggering moral collapse, there is renewed hope for our land. There is hope because more and more churches are beginning to return to a central practice of the past—a powerful corporate prayer meeting. At last we seem to be awakening to the awesome importance of Jesus' words " 'My house shall be called a house of prayer' " (Matt. 21:13, NASB). Although it's still a small minority, growing numbers are rediscovering the incredible power of the churchwide prayer meeting.

Frankly, it seems astounding that modern churches could abandon serious prayer meetings. After all, the New Testament church was literally born in a prayer meeting, and few would doubt that early Christians spent a great deal of their time in united prayer. We all rejoice to read what happened when our fore-fathers prayed; yet in our own generation dynamic weekly prayer meetings have all but disappeared. Although today's church is the most programmed, highly trained, and well funded in history, prayer meetings remain among the most neglected of all church activities. It seems we thought we could somehow organize, promote, or strategize our way into effective Kingdom work. Thank God for grow-ing signs that a new day may be dawning at last.

In this chapter we will examine exciting and prac-tical ways God can raise up dynamic prayer meetings in any congregation. However, it is vital to remember one essential point: powerful prayer meetings are not programs we can orchestrate; they are a genuine relational encounter with God Himself. Furthermore, such meetings do not happen by accident. Church leaders must make a determined commitment to con-sistently lead their congregations into powerful cor-porate prayer. Without the pastors and leaders, it simply will not happen.

### Foundational Steps to Powerful Midweek Prayer Meetings

This section describes eight steps that are founda-tional to God-led prayer meetings. At the end of each step you will find a question to help you evaluate the strength of your church's prayer meetings. The eight evaluation questions can serve as a checklist to help congregations prepare for powerful encounters with God. Do not be overwhelmed by what you read, and do not think you have to embrace all eight steps at once. While conducting scores of prayer conferences, I have seen God mightily bless even the tiniest first steps churches take to strengthen their prayer meetings. Be assured that our merciful Father will take you right where you are and will patiently lead your church into a glorious new relationship with Himself. As you read the following steps, ask God to reveal specific ways He can revolutionize your church's prayer meetings. If you are ready to follow God's leading, neither you nor your congregation will ever be the same.

## Step 1: View the Prayer Meeting as a Relational Encounter with God

As humans, we have a tragic tendency to program so many events that little opportunity exists for a spontaneous relationship with God. In fact, if we are not careful, we can treat prayer meetings as just another program to implement. Spiritual power does not lie in a particular prayer format but in a right relationship with God. Remember that God does not answer prayer; He answers persons who are in right relationships with Him.

Without a strong focus on God Himself, we can program the spiritual life out of a prayer meeting! We can avoid this danger by viewing the prayer meeting primarily as a relational experience with God rather than merely an event to orchestrate. The primary goal in the prayer meeting is to make significant time for people to experience a genuine, spontaneous encounter with God. Be assured that if you as a church leader seek God's direction, He will guide you into a healthy balance between effective planning and close sensitivity to the Spirit of God.

### ✧ *Evaluation Question 1*

Are your prayer meetings so tightly structured that there is no room for the spontaneous leadership of the Holy Spirit?

## Step 2: Promote the Weekly Prayer Meeting as a Top Priority

According to Jeremiah 29:13, our attitude toward prayer must be high intensity and top priority: "Ye shall seek me, and find me, when ye shall search for me with all your heart" (KJV). Churches seldom develop dynamic prayer meetings until prayer becomes a genuine top priority. Such a major emphasis on the weekly prayer meeting requires a definite change in most churches' promotional practices.

To help congregations gain a priority view of the prayer meeting, I suggest a series of brief Bible studies that teach the importance of corporate intercession. It is absolutely vital that we teach congregations the central role of prayer in all great revivals and in all true evangelism. Until congregations fully grasp the importance of corporate intercession, they will continue to view prayer meetings as optional or unimportant.

### ✧ *Evaluation Question 2*

Does your church promote prayer meetings as a top priority?

## Step 3: Prayerfully Plan the Weekly Prayer Meeting

Churches always reveal their real priorities by what they seriously plan, organize, and promote. Today if prayer meetings exist at all, they are often poorly planned and underpromoted. When we give little attention to the prayer meeting, we speak volumes about our true view of prayer.

Thank God this pattern is changing! Growing numbers of churches involve musicians, lay leaders, and the entire staff in planning dynamic weekly prayer meetings. Though this takes work and preparation, such efforts make a huge difference in the churches that take the prayer meeting seriously. However, planning should not be so rigid that you lose sensitivity to God's Spirit. Your planning must leave room for the spontaneous response of God's people. God will teach you the proper balance between planning and spontaneity.

### ✧ *Evaluation Question 3*

What does your present level of planning suggest about your true view of prayer meetings?

## Step 4: Use the Weekly Prayer Meeting to Grow Your People in Intercession

We must face the fact that most modern believers do not know how to pray effectively and that the weekly prayer meeting is the crucial setting in which to teach them. After all, we do not primarily learn to pray by reading books or attending conferences; we learn to pray by praying. If congregations hear weekly prayer teaching, see prayer demonstrated, and then experience it themselves, they soon learn to pray on a different level. Nothing teaches people to pray like praying and hearing others pray.

The prayer meeting is also the time to give your people detailed prayer lists for key issues. An effective prayer list should contain specific requests for each essential category of prayer concerns. (See p. 43 for the seven essential categories for effective prayer lists.) By providing comprehensive prayer lists, we not only teach believers how to intercede but also deliver churches from the practice of praying mostly for health concerns. In this way believers move toward an outward Kingdom focus rather than one that is inward and temporal. Effective prayer lists not only strengthen the weekly prayer meeting but also lead people to more focused prayer in their daily quiet times.

### ✧ Evaluation Question 4
Does your church use prayer meetings to deepen the prayer life of its people?

### Step 5: Schedule Significant Prayer Time in the Weekly Meeting
Although many churches still call their Wednesday-night service a prayer meeting, little time is devoted to actual prayer. The Wednesday-night meeting typically consists of greetings; songs; announcements; a Bible devotion; and perhaps five to seven minutes for prayer, most of which are spent discussing prayer requests. People usually spend so much time talking about prayer requests that they spend almost no time in prayer. As a result, very few churches have anything that even remotely resembles the prayer meetings of the early church or of the great awakenings. This may well be the biggest single reason baptismal ratios have so seriously declined over the past decades.

Modern churches must rethink the amount of time allotted for the weekly prayer meeting. Unfortunately, a great number of churches have gone to a 30-minute schedule. By the time they finish greetings, songs, announcements, Bible teaching, and lists of requests, perhaps only 5 minutes remain for actual prayer. I am not saying that you cannot have a meaningful 30-minute prayer meeting. Indeed, you can if you are prepared to minimize other activities and maximize the time in prayer. I am also not saying that sharing God's Word is less important than

prayer. I strongly encourage briefly sharing Scripture in the prayer meeting, but the primary focus of the prayer meeting must be actual time in prayer.

I suggest that you schedule at least between 45 minutes and one hour for your weekly prayer meeting. In the first 10 to 12 minutes, teach key Scriptures and allow testimonies of answered prayer. That allows 30 to 40 minutes strictly for prayer. Regardless of the length of the prayer meeting, the guiding principle is to schedule most of your time for actual prayer. In most churches this will require major changes, but the results will be worth it.

### ✧ Evaluation Question 5
What percentage of your church prayer meetings' time is spent in actual prayer? Is that enough to qualify your church as a house of prayer?

### Step 6: Focus Prayer More on Eternal than Temporal Issues
In most churches the small amount of time spent in prayer is focused almost entirely on physical needs. Tragically, this means that the prayer focus is almost totally inward and temporal rather than outward and eternal. While God is certainly concerned about physical needs, He also wants us to seek His will and direction for the advancement of His kingdom and our involvement in it. The Father's heart is broken when we endlessly major on temporal concerns to the exclusion of His larger purposes. With a little planning, your church can achieve a healthy balance between eternal and temporal prayer concerns.

### ✧ Evaluation Question 6
What percentage of your prayer meeting is actually focused on eternal Kingdom issues such as lost persons, missionaries, evangelistic efforts, and revival in the church?

### Step 7: Schedule Additional Prayer Meetings with Serious Intercessors
A wise guideline for the Wednesday meeting is to develop strong prayer patterns; yet do not make them so extensive as to eliminate the vast majority of participants. For your more serious intercessors, it is crucial to offer additional prayer meetings of greater intensity and length. In many churches growing numbers of people yearn to go to deeper levels

of prayer, and we must provide the opportunity.

In my church the Wednesday-night meeting includes various seasons, or periods, of powerful prayer. This meeting is not extensive or overwhelming, and the majority of our people feel capable of participating. However, we conduct an additional weekly prayer meeting for those who are willing to pray at length for lost persons, for needs in the church, and for revival in America. The additional prayer meeting, open to everyone, is usually held Sunday nights after church or one night during the week. Although fewer attend this meeting, it is characterized by great power and phenomenal results.

✧ *Evaluation Question 7*

Does your church have at least one weekly prayer meeting that intensely targets lost persons, revival in the church, and spiritual awakening in America?

**Step 8: Promote the Weekly Meeting as a Time of Joy and Life-Changing Power**

When a church conducts powerful corporate prayer meetings, many prayers will be answered, and it will have many reasons to rejoice. Many churches find it appropriate to begin prayer meetings with a time of sharing answered prayers. Nothing fills people with joy and prepares them to pray like hearing recent answers from God. When churches expectantly approach prayer meetings, they quickly discover that true prayer meetings are not dry and dead. Music and worship can be especially powerful ways to enhance prayer meetings. If you choose songs that uplift and foster an atmosphere of expectancy, your midweek prayer meeting will become an incredibly vibrant service. If churches promote prayer meetings as exciting, life-changing events, far more people will attend.

✧ *Evaluation Question 8*

Is your prayer meeting a time of joyful anticipation or a dull formality?

## Patterns for Midweek Prayer Meetings

Let's examine some practical patterns for conducting God-led prayer meetings. For each pattern you will find a general description of the meeting and an outline of the way it usually flows. Ask God to give you

the faith and determination to lead your church to become a powerful house of prayer. If you are willing and obedient, God will lead you on a glorious journey!

As we consider patterns for prayer meetings, remember that no pattern represents a magic formula or a set program. Nor are these three patterns the only ones God uses. As you seek God's direction for your church, He may lead you to any one or a combination of these formats. He may also lead you to a totally different pattern. You don't want to fall into rigid routines. The guiding spiritual principles are to ask God's specific direction and to view each prayer meeting as a relational experience with Him.

In describing the following patterns, we will begin with the most basic and move to the more complex. Each pattern includes a sample format for a one-hour prayer meeting. Listed times are only examples and are not to be viewed as rigid schedules. To design a 30-minute meeting, abbreviate the preliminary activities and reduce the number and length of prayer seasons.

**Pattern 1: Corporate Prayer Meetings**

In this basic yet powerful meeting, participants pray aloud for a wide variety of requests. The majority of time is spent in spontaneous verbal intercession for various issues of concern. This pattern is especially effective in small to midsize churches. To prepare for the meeting, leaders should organize prayer concerns into related categories, with each receiving a focused season of prayer. Although you will not pray through all categories in each meeting, you should be aware of these seven essential categories for prayer.

---

**ESSENTIAL CATEGORIES FOR PRAYER**

1. Lost and backslidden persons
2. Missionaries and missions initiatives
3. Church needs or ministry initiatives
4. Key ministries and denominational needs
5. Revival and spiritual awakening
6. Persecuted believers throughout the world
7. Sick, bereaved, widowed, orphaned, and poor

---

For each category, list several specific prayer requests and distribute copies of the list to those who attend the meeting. You should also provide lists for intercessors who are homebound. Effective weekly prayer lists are invaluable in strengthening members' daily prayer lives. Use discretion in listing the names of lost or backslidden persons on a public prayer list. Consider using only first names.

## SAMPLE FORMAT: CORPORATE PRAYER MEETINGS

7:00 p.m. Welcome and opening hymn or chorus

7:05 p.m. Praise testimonies for answered prayer

7:10 p.m. Scripture reading and opening prayer. Read Scriptures that focus on God's power to answer prayer (for example, Mark 11:22-24; John 14:12-14; 1 John 5:14-15). Share instructions for the prayer time. The pastor or prayer leader should lead an opening prayer and ask people to privately confess any sin God brings to mind. Pause for a few moments of silence to allow participants to search their hearts. (Longer meetings or solemn assemblies may allow ample time for in-depth or even public confession.) The opening prayer time majors on asking for God's forgiveness and for His power in the prayer meeting.

7:17 p.m. First season of prayer: for sick and bereaved (see Jas. 5:15-16). It is usually best to predesignate one or two persons to begin and end each season with corporate prayer. After special needs are mentioned, one of the designated persons begins with corporate prayer. The pastor or leader then asks the people to enter a period of spontaneous prayer for the stated needs of that prayer season. Whether or not they come to the microphone depends on the size of the sanctuary and whether pray-ers can easily be heard. After several minutes of spontaneous prayers, one of the designated persons leads the closing prayer for this season. If no one prays spontaneously, the designated persons should pray for all needs of that prayer season.

7:27 p.m. Second season of prayer: for lost and backslidden (see 2 Pet. 3:9). Especially in smaller churches, prayers for the lost can be offered corporately. Encourage people to bring lists of lost persons. Ask someone to begin with corporate prayer for God's convicting power on these persons. Following the corporate prayer, ask members to spontaneously pray for lost persons—aloud, silently, or in small groups. After several minutes a designated person or a volunteer should lead in corporate prayer to conclude this season.

7:40 p.m. Third season of prayer: for missionaries, special church ministries, denominational needs, revival and spiritual awakening. Briefly call attention to specific needs in this crucial category. Ask one or two persons to be prepared to express corporate prayers for these concerns. One of the designated persons should begin with corporate prayer, after which you encourage others to pray spontaneously. Following several minutes of intercession, one of the designated persons ends the season with corporate prayer.

7:58 p.m. Concluding prayer of agreement (see Matt. 18:19). The pastor or prayer leader asks the congregation to stand and join hands (optional). He leads a concluding prayer that includes all of the prayer categories mentioned. This prayer is offered in the expectant faith that God will answer. The final joint prayer is often one of exuberant praise for God's mercy and power. It is effectively followed by songs of celebration, such as "To God Be the Glory" or "Victory in Jesus." Be sensitive to the possibility that some may want to share insights or testimonies. God often changes lives during prayer meetings! Encourage members to continue in prayer as the Spirit leads them. Provide an adjoining room or another designated area for this purpose.

## Pattern 2: Combined Corporate and Small-Group Prayer Meetings

This meeting generally begins with a time of corporate prayer, continues with a significant period of small-group prayer, and closes with another time of corporate prayer. This pattern is powerful in churches of all sizes.

The initial corporate prayer can be led by one person or as many as five. After the initial period of from 5 to 15 minutes, ask the congregation to gather in small groups of from three to five persons. They can remain in their seats or gather in small groups around the altar. Ask members to take the next 15 to 30 minutes to pray through all requests on their prayer lists. For this reason it is important for prayer lists to be comprehensive. During the group prayer time, emphasize specific prayers for the lost and backslidden. When it is time to end the small-group prayer time, the pastor or leader signals an instrumentalist to softly play one verse of a hymn, signaling the groups to bring their prayers to a close.

The meeting concludes with one or more persons leading corporate prayers that address all key requests of the meeting. It is effective to have everyone stand and join hands as the concluding prayer is offered. It is usually appropriate to end with a song of celebration or praise for God's mercy and power. In this manner the meeting concludes with a powerful sense of anticipation, hope, and praise. Be sensitive to those who desire further prayer. Encourage them to continue praying in an adjoining room or another area designated for that purpose. Many churches quench the Holy Spirit by abruptly ending prayer when people still need to pray.

Pattern 2 has several advantages.

- The congregation experiences a powerful balance between corporate and small-group prayer.
- This pattern maximizes time spent in actual prayer.
- This approach maximizes group participation and affords everyone ample opportunity to pray aloud. This format encourages people to participate rather than merely observe.
- This type of meeting is simple and flows well. Members usually have a strong sense that the meeting is Spirit-directed and God-focused, thereby experiencing a great degree of freedom and spontaneity.

---

### SAMPLE FORMAT: COMBINED CORPORATE AND SMALL-GROUP PRAYER MEETINGS

7:00 p.m. Welcome and opening hymn or chorus

7:05 p.m. Brief testimonies of answered prayer

7:10 p.m. Scripture reading and opening prayer. Read Scriptures that focus on God's power and mercy. Briefly share any special instructions for the prayer time. The pastor or prayer leader should lead an opening prayer and ask participants to search their hearts and confess any sin God brings to mind. Allow a few moments of silence for people to do this (see Pss. 66:18; 139:23-24).

7:20 p.m. Identification of prayer needs. During this period call attention to the various issues for prayer. Emphasize key subjects and encourage the congregation to use the prayer list as a general guide so that their intercession will be focused and thorough.

7:25 p.m. Corporate prayers. Two or three persons lead in corporate prayers for the key subjects on the list. The prayer leaders can be designated, or this time can be left open for spontaneous prayers.

7:35 p.m. Release the congregation into a small-group prayer time. During this extended time period, the groups pray through all of the subjects as God's Spirit directs. This time is especially powerful for praying for the lost by name.

7:55 p.m. Concluding corporate prayers. Ask two or three persons to lead closing corporate prayers for the key issues. During the final prayer you may have people stand and join hands or kneel around the altar. It is often effective to conclude the meeting with a song or a verbal testimony of praise. Be sure to make provisions for those who are led to continue in prayer after the planned time period.

This pattern of prayer meeting also harbors potential difficulties.

- It is possible that some members may be uncomfortable with the significant time in small-group prayer. Some may feel that they are being put on the spot to pray aloud. You can remedy this problem by assuring people that they may pray silently if they so choose.

- Some members have little interest in praying for issues that do not directly affect their daily lives. For such people this kind of meeting will hold little appeal. We must face the fact that increasing the prayer time may actually reduce attendance at some church prayer meetings. However, in many other churches the attendance will increase. In essence we must decide which is more pleasing to God—to have churches with no prayer meetings or to become houses of prayer even if some choose not to participate. Do we really want to let prayerless people dictate whether we have a genuine church prayer meeting? I hope the answer is no!

### Pattern 3: Alternating Seasons of Corporate and Small-Group Prayer

This meeting is characterized by a fairly equal balance of corporate and small-group prayer time. The congregation experiences several seasons of prayer, with corporate and small-group prayer occurring in each season. Intercession flows freely from corporate to small-group prayer as the congregation moves through the various seasons of prayer. This format is usually effective for long prayer meetings and in large congregations.

Typically, such meetings are characterized by four steps. Obviously, in shorter meetings each phase will be limited. Since this type of meeting requires more coordination, a more detailed description of the practical steps is provided.

*Step 1: Opening prayers, Scripture reading, and brief prayer instructions.* After the opening prayer, briefly share Scriptures that relate to key prayer principles. The amount of Scripture largely depends on the planned length of the meeting. If an hour is scheduled, you could conduct a 10-minute Bible lesson and still have significant time for prayer. Again, many churches find it helpful to periodically conduct a series of brief Bible lessons just before the prayer

time. Through this process the congregation receives excellent prayer instruction as well as strong preparation for the prayer meeting. After all, weekly prayer meetings will never be stronger than the individual prayer lives of those who participate. An important goal of the weekly meeting is to grow believers to deeper levels of prayer. This goal is attainable by combining brief prayer teachings with significant periods of prayer.

*Step 2: A period of praise through verbal testimonies, songs, choruses, and prayers of thanksgiving.* Although you have many options for the time of praise, two seem to be the most effective:

1. Ask the congregation to offer verbal prayers of thanks and praise. When congregations get accustomed to spontaneous praise, it is amazing how freely they voice their prayers. After the people have voiced prayers of praise, the pastor or prayer leader offers a powerful corporate prayer of praise and worship to God.

2. Ask for verbal testimonies of praise and answered prayer. After some have shared, lead the congregation in a prayer of praise and thanksgiving. If the testimonies begin to run long, gently bring them to a close so that the time for intercession is not compromised. If no one testifies aloud, the pastor or someone appointed proceeds with a corporate prayer of praise and thanksgiving.

*Step 3: A period of confession and cleansing to prepare the congregation for prayer (see Prov. 28:13; 1 John 1:9).* A vital key to a powerful meeting is helping people spiritually prepare for prayer. Since some may not have the chance or inclination to prepare, conduct a period of silent reflection during which you ask the people to confess any known sin. Just a few minutes of reflection can allow God to bring obvious sins to the minds of the people so that they can prepare spiritually to pray. Two-hour prayer meetings allow more time for in-depth confession and repentance. More thorough cleansing is encouraged through periodic churchwide solemn assemblies.

*Step 4: The primary time of intercession.* Lead the congregation through a specific season of intercession for each prayer subject. As the prayer leader introduces the subject of each prayer season, he should briefly state some of the key points. Encourage the congregation to use the prayer lists for guidance in the seasons of prayer. Ask the people to gather in groups of from three to five as they prepare for intercession. Some may want to stay seated in groups while others gather at the altar.

The following guidelines will help this time go smoothly.

1. Encourage prayer groups to pray aloud, but allow freedom for some individuals to pray silently.

2. Ask people to pray loud enough to be heard by their group but not by the whole room. This will ensure an orderly meeting.

3. When it is time to end each season of prayer, an instrumentalist should softly play one verse of an appropriate hymn. Usually, the prayer leader can simply nod to the instrumentalist when it is time to end each season of prayer. I suggest a minimum of from 8 to 10 minutes for each season; longer is usually better. Be sure to have enough requests on your prayer list so that people will not run out of prayer needs.

4. As people end their small-group prayers, the leader or someone appointed should voice a corporate prayer for the issues addressed in that particular season. At this point you are ready to move immediately to the next season of prayer.

5. The prayer leader briefly shares the focus of the next season, calls attention to the prayer list, and again releases members into small-group prayer. Follow the same pattern throughout each season of prayer. Do not spend excessive time introducing the different prayer seasons.

6. The prayer leader closes the meeting with a final prayer of praise for God's anticipated answers. During the concluding prayer, ask the entire congregation to stand or gather at the altar. It is especially moving if the worship leader closes by leading songs such as "God Is So Good," "To God Be the Glory," or "Victory in Jesus."

Each week you could rotate some of the categories of focus. In this manner you will effectively cover a complete range of issues every four to six weeks. One advantage of this approach is its flexibility for

---

**SAMPLE FORMATS: ALTERNATING SEASONS OF CORPORATE AND SMALL-GROUP PRAYER**

### One-Hour Prayer Meeting

6:50 Prelude of worship music

7:00 Welcome, introduction, and opening prayer

7:05 Hymns, testimonies, or corporate prayers of praise

7:15 Scripture reading, confession, and preparation for prayer

7:25 Season of prayer for sick, bereaved, and other crises (corporate and small groups)

7:35 Season of prayer for the lost, unchurched, church ministries, missionaries (corporate and small groups)

7:50 Season of prayer for revival and spiritual awakening (corporate and small groups)

8:00 Closing prayer of celebration (corporate)

### Two-Hour Prayer Meeting

6:45 Prelude of worship music

7:00 Welcome, introduction, and opening prayer

7:05 Period of congregational worship and soloists

7:15 Season of testimonies and prayers of praise

7:25 Soloist or group worship song

7:30 Scripture reading for confession and repentance

7:35 Prayers of confession and repentance (Congregation is led through spiritual cleansing.)

7:50 Songs of praise for God's cleansing

7:55 Reading of prayer promises

8:00 Season of prayer for crises and personal needs (corporate and small groups)

8:15 Season of prayer for lost, unchurched, and local church needs (corporate and small groups)

8:30 Season of prayer for city, for regional revival, for missionaries and denominational initiatives (corporate and small groups)

8:45 Season of prayer for revival and spiritual awakening (corporate and small groups)

9:00 Closing prayers and worship (corporate)

churches of all sizes. I have seen God mightily anoint this pattern in prayer meetings ranging from 30 to 3,000 people. The Lord will greatly bless the inclusion of appropriate music and worship.

## Practical Reminders for Corporate Prayer Meetings

As you plan corporate prayer meetings, keep these points in mind.

1. It is not always necessary to designate persons to lead corporate prayers. Congregations can leave prayer meetings open to the spontaneous prompting of God's Spirit. In churches where people readily pray aloud, the spontaneous approach is usually more effective. However, in many churches prayer meetings flow more smoothly if some are designated beforehand to give prayer leadership at strategic points. It is not unspiritual to ask godly people to prepare to lead prayer at a weekly meeting.

2. When you open the floor for spontaneous prayer, you may want to limit it to three or four persons for each prayer season. Otherwise, you can easily spend all your time on one subject and fall into a repetitive pattern. After a designated person opens with a corporate prayer, ask two or three others to spontaneously voice prayers as God's Spirit directs. This way there is freedom for spontaneous prayer; yet the spiritual leaders still have general direction of the meeting. However, sometimes you will sense God's leading to focus the whole meeting on only one or two urgent subjects. Again, the guiding principles are close sensitivity to the Spirit of God and a flexible schedule that allows God's Spirit to work.

3. It is not necessary to ask a different person to lead each corporate prayer. In some smaller churches the pastor and one or two others may be the only ones comfortable with praying corporately. Even if the pastor is the only corporate intercessor, churches can still have powerful prayer meetings. If necessary, the pastor can corporately pray for each category and ask the congregation to join him silently. (In historic awakenings lengthy pastoral prayers were common.)

4. There is no set number of subjects you must cover in the prayer meeting. In fact, fewer seasons of prayer can allow a more intense focus on each category. Fewer seasons of prayer are especially important if you schedule only a 30-minute prayer time. The length and number of seasons are largely dictated by the planned length of the prayer meeting. In our examples we have described mostly one-hour prayer meetings. Obviously, in shorter meetings it is necessary to adjust both the length and number of prayer seasons.

5. Choose permanent subjects that are addressed each week and other subjects that rotate from week to week. This way you thoroughly cover all key issues at least every six weeks. Modern congregations need to learn to intercede for the full range of Kingdom issues. For permanent subjects I suggest lost persons, missionaries, crisis needs, revival, and spiritual awakening.

## Answers to Commonly Asked Questions

Although we cannot cover all questions in this chapter, we can address a few of the most common.

### How Do We Motivate People to Attend Wednesday-Night Prayer Meetings?
- By presenting biblical teachings on prayer
- By consistently promoting the prayer meeting as an essential priority
- By planning inspiring and uplifting elements such as testimonies and music
- By sharing during the Sunday-morning worship service testimonies of ways God is answering the prayers of those who attend
- By emphasizing how people will learn to pray by attending the prayer meeting
- By emphasizing how people can experience spiritual growth by attending the prayer meeting

### How Do We Encourage People to Look Outward in Their Praying?
- By providing specific, written prayer requests for a broad range of issues
- By teaching participants how to be effective intercessors
- By teaching participants what will happen as they pray for others
- By scheduling seasons of prayer that specifically focus on a variety of issues

## How Do We Maintain Focus in the Prayer Meeting?

- By providing a comprehensive prayer list for each category of focus
- By utilizing seasons of prayer to address the various issues
- By the leadership of the pastor or prayer leader
- By asking certain persons to pray for specific issues

## How Do We Keep Prayer Meetings Fresh and Spontaneous?

- By prayerfully planning each prayer meeting
- By regularly changing the format as God's Spirit directs
- By utilizing personal testimonies and reports of answered prayer
- By gathering with the staff to ask God's blessing in the prayer meetings

## How Do We Encourage People to Pray Aloud?

- By modeling praying aloud
- By consistently encouraging people to pray aloud
- By periodically offering Scripture lessons that teach people how to pray
- By consistently assigning various persons to pray aloud, who over time will become more comfortable
- By emphasizing the sincerity of prayer rather than the way it sounds

As churches commit to serious corporate prayer, other questions will certainly surface. However, most questions can be answered by a thorough application of the eight foundational steps mentioned earlier. As we further consider corporate prayer, we must address three additional patterns with enormous importance for today's society. These three patterns are small-group prayer meetings, evangelistic prayer meetings, and prayer meetings for spiritual awakening.

## Small-Group Prayer Meetings

One of today's most exciting trends is the growing number of small-group prayer meetings. Such meetings can be conducted in a variety of ways. I will focus on the type of meeting in which a small group gathers for an extended time in fervent prayer. A group of from 3 to 12 persons gathers for one or two hours of prayer and sharing. Although there is no rigid format, the group generally spends time in four different types of prayer:

1. Praise
2. Confession
3. Petition
4. Intercession

Time is also given for sharing personal needs or testimonies. However, the major focus in these groups is on prayer. The goal in the meeting is to allow enough time for the group to experience a powerful encounter with God.

### Special Benefits of Small-Group Prayer Meetings

1. The prayer group does not place a brief time limit on meeting with God. We limit God when we try to squeeze Him into our busy schedules, seeking Him only at our convenience. In small-group meetings participants can experience a genuine relational encounter with God rather than just quickly praying through a list.
2. God uses the meeting to teach people to pray on a deeper level. In this type of meeting, group members have time to experience deep levels of all four prayer types. As participants pray and hear others praying, they experience phenomenal spiritual growth. Small-group prayer meetings are a powerful form of discipleship.
3. Small-group prayer meetings allow adequate time for participants to get thoroughly clean before God. It is unrealistic to think we can do serious biblical confession and repentance in a brief two-minute time of silence. Small-group prayer allows an opportunity to take the group through a significant time of cleansing. In this manner the intercession can have genuine spiritual power (see Jas. 5:16).
4. Small-group prayer meetings allow time for participants to pray effectively for large numbers of lost persons by name. When a group is willing to commit significant time, it can pray for greater numbers, often at a deeper level of fervency. Extremely brief prayer times limit both the amount and the intensity of intercession.
5. Small-group prayer meetings provide the opportu-

nity and training to pray consistently for revival and spiritual awakening. Many people do not know how to pray effectively for spiritual awakening. In small-group prayer meetings participants learn the principles of powerful intercession.

6. Small-group prayer meetings engender the deep fellowship and mutual support that are lacking in many churches. When people share deep needs and fervently pray together, they experience the genuine biblical fellowship for which many modern believers are starving.

**A Basic Format for Small-Group Prayer Meetings**
Before I share a general format, I again stress that we should never be so set on a particular pattern that we lose sensitivity to God's direction. At its heart any prayer meeting should be a relationship with God, not a program. The following pattern is one frequently used in small-group settings.

### SAMPLE FORMAT: SMALL-GROUP PRAYER MEETINGS

1. Opening prayer and sharing time (10–15 mins.). Participants share needs and/or testimonies.
2. Praise and thanksgiving (10–15 mins.). The group expresses prayers of praise and thanks.
3. Confession and cleansing (10–15 mins.). The prayer leader takes the group through a process of confession and repentance.
4. Intercession (30–40 mins.). The group prays for a wide range of needs. Special focus is given to praying for the lost as well as for revival and spiritual awakening.
5. Processing what God has said (10–15 mins.). The group shares insights or impressions gained in the prayer meeting.

This pattern is one God powerfully blesses in small-group settings. Groups do not always have to meet for lengthy prayer times. To carry out specific prayer strategies, many churches are led to use a variety of small-group prayer strategies.

## Evangelistic Prayer Meetings

Recently, we have witnessed an explosion of interest in the term *prayer evangelism*. Prayer evangelism is the total integration of prayer into every evangelistic effort, with prayer becoming the central element rather than merely an appendage. Prayer evangelism encompasses a wide range of prayer strategies, including evangelistic prayer meetings, prayerwalking, list praying, prayer triads, Lighthouses of Prayer, Houses of Prayer Everywhere, and Praying for You. Many of these are described in chapter 5.

In my own life and church God has used evangelistic praying far more than anything else. In 1990 we started our first evangelistic prayer meetings and began praying specifically for 60 lost persons by name. In less than four months 45 of the 60 had been gloriously saved! After using various evangelistic strategies for many years, I have found that combining evangelistic prayer with ongoing outreach efforts is the most effective strategy. When churches combine serious evangelistic prayer with today's excellent evangelism strategies, we will indeed see the next great awakening!

Although several strategies fall into the category of evangelistic praying, we will focus on prayer meetings to intercede for the lost by name. In an evangelistic prayer meeting the primary purpose is fervent intercession for lost persons and for the believers who are seeking to reach them. In past great awakenings, evangelistic prayer meetings were a huge factor in the massive flood of salvations. Weekly church prayer meetings were characterized by intense prayer for lost persons by name and by large numbers of lay leaders who led in prayer. In the past several decades we have witnessed a tragic move away from this type of prayer meeting. Surely it is no coincidence that during the same period our baptismal ratios have dramatically declined. Today God is definitely drawing churches back to evangelistic prayer meetings.

God is mightily using the following three patterns of evangelistic prayer meetings.

### Devoting the Midweek Prayer Meeting to Evangelistic Intercession
Although this approach may not be practical for every church, some churches are mature enough to embrace such a weekly meeting. When past genera-

tions embraced evangelistic praying, they saw an explosion of salvation and a genuine revival among God's people. In this type of prayer meeting you might ask the congregation to cluster in small groups throughout the sanctuary, though some corporate prayers can and should be offered.

For many churches a more practical pattern is to devote one prayer meeting each month to evangelistic praying. Especially on that night encourage members to bring lists of lost persons and to come prepared for a time of intense prayer. It can also be helpful to ask people to fast on this night. Incredible results can come from this type of emphasis. In many cases you will see such results that your people will want to do this every week.

### Small-Group Evangelistic Prayer Meetings

This meeting is generally not conducted at the weekly churchwide prayer time. Although the whole church should be invited, this is a special meeting for those who feel a strong burden to fervently pray for the lost. Such meetings are usually more intense and longer than most churchwide prayer meetings. Remember, large numbers do not necessarily bring phenomenal results. Even groups as small as 2 or 3 can experience miraculous power and results. When groups grow much larger than 10, consider dividing into smaller groups so that everyone has ample opportunity to pray. When you pray in smaller groups, you can also divide prayer lists and pray more effectively for greater numbers of people. Such meetings can be conducted in churches, private homes, schools, or anywhere God leads.

### Evangelistic Prayer Meetings
### During Soul-Winning Visitation

One of today's most hopeful signs is the increasing integration of prayer and evangelistic strategies. Although most evangelistic programs already include the enlistment of prayer partners to intercede for teams that are visiting, a powerful additional strategy is to ask the prayer partners to actually gather and pray for the lost while the teams are witnessing. Such a practice adds much more prayer to soul-winning initiatives yet in no way interferes with the structure of any evangelistic program. This type of corporate prayer is far more focused and powerful than when people pray merely on their own (see

Matt. 18:19; Acts 2:1). Furthermore, don't limit evangelistic prayer meetings to prayer partners, because some from the general congregation are often willing to gather and pray for soul-winning teams that are visiting.

In this type of meeting, intercessors should specifically pray for the following elements.

- Power and protection for persons witnessing
- Conviction, repentance, and salvation of specific lost persons
- Discipleship and growth of those who have been saved
- Sweeping revival in the church
- Special needs in intercessors' lives

It is usually best to conduct evangelistic prayer meetings at the church and to have the prayer groups arrive at the same time as the soul-winning teams. The prayer groups should begin praying for the soul-winning teams while they meet for previsit training (usually from 6:30 to 7:00 p.m.). As the teams visit, the prayer groups can shift their praying toward individual lost persons (7:00–8:00 p.m.). At that point the prayer groups can either conclude their praying or pray for the discipleship of recent converts and for genuine revival in the church (8:00–8:30 p.m.).

The following five steps have proved crucial to conducting evangelistic prayer groups.

1. Someone should agree to serve as the leader or coordinator of the prayer meeting. This person gives general direction in the prayer time and keeps people informed of meeting times and places. The leader also sees that prayer lists are updated and correlates prayer times with evangelistic efforts.

2. Ask group members to prepare for the meeting by spending time in personal confession and repentance. Participants can do this before coming to the meeting, or you can schedule preparation time just before the group begins to pray. This step is essential because it spiritually prepares the group to pray. Many prayer meetings have little power because of intercessors' unconfessed sin (see Ps. 66:18).

3. Keep a specific, up-to-date list of lost persons and pray for them by name. Never forget that specific prayer has far greater power than prayers that are general or unfocused.

4. Take time to thoroughly pray for each person and be sensitive to special prompting from God's Spirit. When we mechanically rush through a prayer list, the meeting's power is greatly reduced. If we are sensitive to God's Spirit, He often gives a special burden for certain persons that varies from day to day.

5. Combine prayers with consistent efforts to witness to lost persons. Witnessing efforts can be accomplished by those in the prayer group, the pastor, or members of outreach teams. God grants incredible results when evangelistic prayer is combined with consistent soul-winning. Prayer and soul-winning must be combined. It is not enough to do one without the other.

It is impossible to overstate the importance of churches' returning to powerful evangelistic prayer meetings. May God help us return to prayer as the foundational strategy in all we do! After all, if our praying is small and inconsistent, then our efforts invariably lack God's fullest power. The great beauty of prayer evangelism is its simplicity. Any church can embrace evangelistic praying, no matter what its size or age breakdown. Even if only two or three persons in your church are willing to participate, you already have enough to begin!

## Prayer Meetings for Revival and Spiritual Awakening

Few believers doubt that society's greatest need is genuine revival and spiritual awakening. Yet many Christians confess that they do not know how to effectively pray for spiritual awakening. In pastoring and conducting many conferences, I have found it extremely important to give believers specific points for biblical intercession. At least 10 specific elements can be observed in biblical and historical awakenings. These form the basis of 10 focused prayers that leaders can provide their congregations to deepen their prayers for revival and spiritual awakening.

The following 10 prayers cover the key elements that are crucial to any great awakening. However, the specific prayers are not meant to be a formula to be prayed in a rote, mechanical manner. Although the 10 prayers serve as a guide, the Holy Spirit must lead people to pray these prayers in their own words and in their own contexts.

1. Ask God to pour out deep conviction of sin, spiritual brokenness, a holy fear of God, and genuine repentance among His people. There will be no revival without these elements, and only God can produce them in His people. After all, we cannot program or manufacture genuine brokenness and repentance (see 2 Cor. 7:10).

2. Pray for deep cleansing, genuine repentance, and spiritual power to engulf pastors and Christian leaders (see Eph. 6:14-20). Revival and spiritual awakening are extremely unlikely without a mighty move of God in pastors and Christian leaders. Renewed pastors are crucial to a move of God in our day.

3. Pray for God to pour out spiritual hunger and unite His people in fervent intercession. God must grant people genuine faith and the fervent desire for prayer. With all our promotion and programming, we cannot produce a genuine prayer movement (see Phil. 2:13).

4. Pray for God to bring loving unity in our churches and deep harmony among our churches. Many churches need healing among members, and some need to stop competing with other churches (see John 13:35).

5. Pray for God to fill His people with a passion to see people saved (see Rom. 9:1-3). Only God can give a genuine burden for souls. Until God's people intensely pray for the lost and aggressively win souls, revival will tarry. Be sure you constantly pray for many lost persons by name.

6. Pray for God to give His people a passion for missions and starting churches. Great revivals produce an explosion of mission projects, new ministries, and new church starts. Only God can grant a genuine passion for missions (see Matt. 28:18-20).

7. Pray for God to call thousands into ministry, missions, and Christian service. Many churches are dying for a lack of soul-winners, teachers, and church workers. Furthermore, we can start only as many churches as we have church planters to start them (see Matt. 9:37).

8. Pray for God to pour out His Spirit like a mighty, purifying flood. Ask God to purify our motives as we pray for revival. It is possible to pray for revival for selfish or ambitious reasons. Our motives must be solely for God's glory and

the increase of His kingdom. We must not pray for revival to solve our own problems or to make our church successful in the eyes of people (see Jas. 4:2-3).

9. Pray for a mighty move of conviction and salvation to touch communities of cultural influence. Some key examples are Hollywood actors and producers, government officials, educators, media representatives, and the music industry (see 1 Tim. 2:1-2). Provide specific lists for your congregation.

10. Specifically pray for God to pour out His Spirit to a greater degree than He did in America in 1857–58 and in Wales in 1904, when 10 percent of Wales's population was saved in five months. Ask God for a modern-day Pentecost (see Matt. 11:20-24; John 14:13-14).

I strongly suggest that churches pray for spiritual awakening as part of their weekly prayer meetings. It is also important to periodically (monthly or quarterly) call special prayer meetings to focus entirely on revival and spiritual awakening. As congregations pray for spiritual awakening, they should follow the same biblical patterns we have described for other types of prayer meetings.

Remember these key points about praying for revival and spiritual awakening.

- When your people pray for revival and spiritual awakening, provide the 10 specific prayers described above to help your congregation focus and pray biblically. Encourage your congregation to take the requests home to use in their personal prayer times.
- Under each of the 10 prayers you may want to list points for additional focus. Be as specific as possible by listing the names of Christian leaders, government leaders, cultural leaders, and so forth.
- As you pray for revival and spiritual awakening, embrace a threefold focus by praying for your own life and church, your city and region, and the nation and world.

## Corporate Prayer: A Lifeline of Hope, A Strategy for Change

Over the past decades modern believers have likely developed more programs and tools than all of Christianity before us. Yet at the same time, we have seen our baptisms stagnate and the nation go into a shocking spiritual free-fall. By God's grace we are at last awakening to the essential element so long neglected. God's people are beginning to humble themselves in serious corporate prayer as more realize that without fervent prayer no strategy has any hope of shaking this wicked nation. We are further awakening to the fact that God's power is released in corporate prayer as in no other way.

I issue a passionate plea to every pastor, church leader, and lay leader: please do not let anything discourage you from starting powerful prayer meetings in your church. By God's grace even the weakest church can take significant steps toward serious corporate prayer. Whatever it takes, let us awaken from our prayerless activities and return to God through corporate prayer. Let us once again embrace the impassioned plea of Jesus' disciples in Luke 11:1, "Lord, teach us to pray" (KJV)!

# CREATIVE IDEAS *for* PRAYER MINISTRY

## PHIL MIGLIORATTI

The role of mobilizing and guiding people into prayer is a significant one. You become a servant the Lord uses to reveal the mysteries and applications of His Word and to guide families and ministries onto the path of His perfect will. May the Lord release many great blessings on you and those you lead into a greater understanding of and experience with prayer. This chapter provides ideas and inspiration you can use in a variety of groups and gatherings for years to come.

The best and most creative prayer idea is always the one God selects or creates. Always begin your prayer-idea search with prayer, allowing the Spirit of God to determine your agenda and to reveal your focus or format. Ask God to direct you to a specific idea described in this chapter or to use one of the ideas to spark a new idea or a different application. Be open to His direction; He may want you to customize what you read here for His purposes in your church.

Each creative prayer idea provides—

- a description of the basic idea, indicating its purpose and benefits;
- the target audience the idea should suit most effectively;
- the process that will assist you in implementing the idea in your setting;

- contact information that will connect you with additional resources relevant to the particular idea, when applicable.

Recommend this resource to others who lead prayer. If you are mentoring someone into prayer leadership, ask them to read and pray over this chapter and to discuss with you what they think would be a God-idea for your group, ministry, or congregation.

Every member of the church needs to be instructed in the basics of a power-filled life of prayer. Beyond that, everyone called into the ministry of prayer should expect further instruction, training, and equipping for their role of service.

Prayer connects us to the God who created the universe—the God who has the authority to touch the lives of our neighbors and neighborhoods, the desire to change the lives of families and communities, the power to alter the course of nations and history. You may embark on no greater journey than to gather; equip; and lead men, women, youth, children, small groups, and congregations into the journey of prayer, talking and listening to the Master.

To find out what God is doing so that you may join Him, pray. Pray with others. Pray for others—without ceasing.

## Directory of Prayer-Ministry Ideas

**CHILDREN/YOUTH**

## Idea 1: Baby-Dedication Blessings

### Description

Most congregations look forward to baby dedications, when newborns are committed to God in the presence of their church family. This is an opportunity to teach the children in the congregation that God loves them and to demonstrate the role of prayer and the importance of a family blessing.

### Target Audience
Churchwide

### Implementation Process

1. Incorporate into your baby dedication an explanation and an expression of praying blessings on family members.
2. Explain that from the beginning of the Old Testament, God blessed His people, and His people blessed those they loved. Today our words of blessing have a spiritual impact on the persons we pray for.
3. Choose from these possibilities.

- Explain to the parents the power of a blessing as you plan the ceremony. Ask them to pray a blessing over their child during the dedication. They may pray extemporaneously, from a written prayer, or from Scripture.
- Allow the parents to invite their families to surround them at the conclusion of the dedication. A believing family member prays a prayer of blessing.
- Invite the children of the church to surround the couple and their child as you pray ("Let the children come").
- Arrange for another church couple to stand with them, offering prayers for the mother, the father, and the child.
- As you pray a blessing for the child, invite the congregation to stand and extend a hand in your direction, as a sign of their agreement and their desire that the Lord will bless this child and this family.

## Idea 2: Beach-Ball Prayer

### Description

Learning to pray for the nations of the world becomes fun when children toss a beach-ball globe around the room.

### Target Audiences
Children, families

### Implementation Process

1. Purchase a beach-ball globe of the world from a teaching-supply store.
2. Begin by explaining that God loves all people, no matter where they live, what color they are, or what language they speak.
3. Memorize together Matthew 28:19, " 'Go and make disciples of all nations, baptizing them in the name of the Father and of the Son and of the Holy Spirit' " (NIV).
4. Sing "Jesus Loves the Little Children."
5. Thank God that He loves all people: people we don't know, people we can't reach, and people who are hard to like.
6. Explain that everyone will have an opportunity to throw and catch the beach ball. Say: When it comes to you, catch it or grab it. Then look at the nation your right thumb is touching or is close to.
7. The children should pray for the people of that nation. Thank God for creating and loving the people who live there. Thank Him that they are unlike any other people. Ask the Lord to bless all Christians in that country and to help them tell their neighbors about Jesus. Ask God to help the children, the poor, and people hurt by floods or earthquakes.
8. Toss the ball to someone who has not yet had an opportunity to pray.
9. Purchase from one of the following sources a resource that contains information about the nations of the world. If the material is age-level appropriate, have the child who catches the ball read about the country. If the child is too young, have an adult sit with him or her so that the two can read about the country together. Ask each child to share two or three items about the people. Then have them pray.

**Contact or Resource Information**
- *On-Mission Prayer Map*. Call (770) 410-6300.
- *You Can Change the World; You Can Change the World, Vol. 2*. Call (800) 798-ACMC (2262).

# Idea 3: Joyride

**Description**
Jump into a vehicle, turn on the music, go somewhere fun, pray, then play! The purpose is to have a blast while making a difference in prayer.

**Target Audience**
Any group, especially youth

**Implementation Process**
1. Utilize these ingredients.
   - A fun activity—the beach, water park, concert, skiing, zoo, or museum
   - A bunch of people—a youth group, small group, or Sunday School class
   - A vehicle—a car, van, or bus
   - Joyful noise—songs and prayers of thanks, gratitude, and happiness as you travel
2. Make sure participants understand that this activity includes playing *and* praying! Although guests should be made welcome, regulars need to know what will take place so that they can make wise decisions about whom to invite.
3. Promote with a theme like "We're Gonna Pray and Go MAD!" (Make a Difference).
4. When the group has arrived—
   - assemble in huddles;
   - pray about the purpose of the joyride: "Lord, grant us a safe, fun time, but also empower us to pray against Satan's strongholds and the darkness in our town."
5. As the group begins the journey—
   - lead in a joyful song of praise;
   - pray, "Lord, give us eyes to see the needs of the people and neighborhoods as we drive";
   - ask individuals in cars and vans or pairs on a bus to pray.
6. On the way or on-site—
   - plan to stop at several locations that need prayer—schools, sites of tragedy, city gates, or seats of authority such as city hall;
   - stop and prayerwalk around the building.

7. When you've arrived at your final, fun location—
   - enjoy yourself, but stop every 15 minutes and pray for those around you;
   - plan to pray at a designated location at the top of every hour.
8. Before you return home—
   - give thanks;
   - share impressions and insights;
   - take photos that can be used as prayer-request cards later.

# Idea 4: Prayer Aerobics for Children

**Description**
Children are ready and willing to pray but often need an active method to keep their attention. Movement, speaking aloud, and expressing emotion engage the entire person and connect with a variety of learning-style preferences. Gather the children in a place where they can make noise and move around without disturbing other groups.

**Target Audiences**
Children, families

**Implementation Process**
1. Ask the group how to spell the word *pray*. Then explain this acrostic:
   P = Praise
   R = Return
   A = Ask
   Y = Yes
2. Make a poster for each letter. Volunteers can hold the posters during each section.
3. Select a Scripture verse for each letter. Shorten longer verses to be age-level appropriate.
   P = Praise. Praise the Lord!
   R = Return. Return to God.
   A = Ask. Ask God anything.
   Y = Yes. Say yes to God's will.
4. Select a different posture or action for each segment.
   P = Raise hands in the air, telling God how great He is while you smile, laugh, and jump with joy.
   R = Kneel, asking God to forgive you for your sins, things you have done wrong.
   A = Stand with hands outstretched and palms up,

ready to receive God's blessings and instructions.

Y = Step to the front or kneel at the altar, telling the Lord that you are ready to follow Him and obey what He tells you to do.

5. Play Christian praise music in the background. As a transition from one segment (letter) to the next, sing a well-known song together.

## Idea 5: Praying at the Pole

### Description
On a specified day at a specified time, youth are challenged to gather around their school's flagpole to pray. This visible witness to faith in God and the power of prayer affords youth opportunities to talk with their friends about their faith.

### Target Audience
Youth

### Implementation Process
1. Plan to participate in the national See You at the Pole initiative, usually held in early September.
   • Inform your congregation and youth that your church will support this effort.
   • Gather youth to provide information and to talk about their interest or apprehension.
   • Schedule a follow-up meeting to discuss their experience and hopes for the future.
2. Schedule your own local Praying at the Pole initiative.
   • Begin by sharing the vision with several other youth leaders so that many students can be involved.
   • Determine the best date, time, and format.
   • Discuss the need to inform the school. Seek as much cooperation as possible.
   • Schedule a youth prayer jam.
   —Share the vision with the students in the cooperating ministries.
   —Explain the power of praying for friends by name.
   —Teach the basics of asking friends for prayer requests.
   —Spend time praying in small groups for friends.
   —Encourage youth to carry a list of their friends' requests.

—Provide opportunities to talk about their friends and pray for them in meetings before and after Praying at the Pole.

### Contact or Resource Information
• See You at the Pole. Call (817) 447-7526; email *pray@syatp.com*; visit *www.syatp.com*.
• *Praying Your Friends to Christ Training Guide* and *Praying Your Friends to Christ Tract.* Call (866) 407-NAMB; visit *www.namb.net/catalog*.
• *An Awesome Way to Pray.* Write to Customer Service Center; One LifeWay Plaza; Nashville, TN 37234-0113; call (800) 458-2772; fax (615) 251-5933; email *customerservice@lifeway.com*; order online at *www.lifeway.com*; or visit a LifeWay Christian Store.

**EVENTS**

## Idea 6: Come to Church Hungry

### Description
The Bible teaches us to pray; it also commands us to fast. Asking the congregation to skip one or two meals before a church service is a gentle way to introduce some members to fasting.

### Target Audience
Churchwide

### Implementation Process
1. Ask the Holy Spirit for a prayer focus.
   • Preparing to celebrate the Lord's Supper
   • Praying for lost neighbors you have invited to church
   • Seeking a personal breakthrough
   • Anticipating a solemn assembly
   • Making a decision about a crucial churchwide matter
   • Facing a church problem or conflict
   • Interceding for seriously ill church members
2. Prepare the congregation.
   • Bulletin announcement
   • Phone calls
   • Letter or cards

3. Explain the purpose of fasting while praying.
   - Fasting requires discipline and sacrifice.
   - Fasting reminds us that we are dependent on the Lord.
   - Fasting enables our minds to focus and listen better.
   - Fasting is a weapon of spiritual warfare; we are empowered.
   - Fasting is nothing to brag about; just do it.
4. Explain the options of fasting.
   - Do not eat any food for a set time; drink only water.
   - Eat only a simple meal of bread and water.
   - Begin the evening prior to the event or skip breakfast.
5. Help parents inform, instruct, and involve their children and young people.
   - *Inform.* Children and youth need to know that biblical prayer includes fasting.
   - *Instruct.* Make it clear that the purpose of fasting is neither to appease an angry God nor to use pain as motivation or punishment. Fasting helps us (1) focus on God rather than food; (2) be obedient to Jesus' command that we keep asking, seeking, and knocking; (3) seek to serve by hearing the Lord's voice and knowing and obeying His will; and (4) trust the Lord with all our hearts, souls, and minds.
   - *Involve.* Talk together about ways all family members should participate. Each one may want to sacrifice something different, such as one meal, a certain food, TV, or music. Allow each member to keep the particular sacrifice secret, but pray for one another as a means of keeping accountable. Declaring your fast does not violate Jesus' command to fast in secret. He was speaking against those who reveal their fasting to bring attention and glory to themselves. Make this sacrifice an action of joyful obedience so that your children are eager to do it again.

## Idea 7: Concert of Prayer

### Description

A concert of prayer calls the entire congregation to spend one or two hours in prayer. Participants gather in small groups and pray for a specific prayer assignment. Benefits include mobilizing the congregation to pray and teaching prayer by pairing inexperienced pray-ers with veteran intercessors. A concert of prayer can be held in lieu of an evening service, on a weekend, or as a special occasion.

### Target Audience

Churchwide

### Implementation Process

1. Select a general theme, for example, "Let's Give Thanks to Our God!" Other possibilities include the following.
   - Use a section of Scripture such as Psalm 23 or Proverbs 3:5-10, allowing each aspect of the teaching to become a focal point of prayer.
   - Pray geographically for lives, families, neighbors, city, nation, and world.
   - Connect various doctrines: creation (praise), salvation (confession), redemption (forgiveness), sanctification (Holy Spirit-empowered maturity), and consummation (the glorious return of Christ).
   - Adopt a theme from the Lord's Prayer or the Beatitudes.
2. Divide the theme into several segments, each with a specific focus.
   - Give thanks for God: extol His attributes.
   - Give thanks to God: express gratitude for answered prayers.
   - Give thanks for hope in Christ: intercede for unsaved friends.
   - Give thanks for the power of the Holy Spirit: offer petitions for persons who are sick or distressed.
3. Select a format. For example:
   6:00 Song of praise
   6:15 Prayer
   Welcome
   Greet one another
   6:25 Thematic focus
   Brief instructions
   Gather in groups
   6:35 Prayers and praise
   - Give thanks for God: extol His attributes.
   - Song of praise
   - Give thanks to God: express gratitude for answered prayers.
   - Song of praise

- Give thanks for hope in Christ: intercede for unsaved friends.
- Song of praise
- Give thanks for the power of the Holy Spirit: offer petitions for persons who are sick or distressed.

8:00 Dismiss

4. Lead the concert of prayer.
   - Praise leader and prayer leader remain visible at the front.
   - Ask the congregation to gather in groups of from four to six persons.
   - Place thematic songs and hymns of praise between each segment. The prayer leader should explain that when a song is begun, it is time to move from prayer to praise.
   - Prayer leader guides groups from one topic to the next, giving brief explanations or suggestions. Trust the Holy Spirit to illuminate participants when it is their opportunity to pray.
   - Prayer leader encourages those who are comfortable praying aloud to be brief and to focus on the topic. The leader also reminds those who are not comfortable praying aloud that the Lord listens to the simplest prayer.

**Contact or Resource Information**
Concerts of Prayer, International. Write to P.O. Box 770; New Providence, NJ 07974; call (877) NOW-HOPE; email *COPI@aol.com*; visit *www.nationalprayer.org*.

## Idea 8: March for Jesus/Praise Parade

**Description**
A praise parade is a glorified prayerwalk! It takes the congregation outside the church facility and into the community to give God glory and praise. Our neighbors are influenced by the unity of the church and impressed by the joy and love we express for our Lord. Praise and prayer lead to evangelism.

**Target Audience**
Churchwide

**Implementation Process**
1. A praise parade can be held any time of the year, but coordinate with the plans of the national March for Jesus movement.

2. If your congregation is joining the citywide March for Jesus, the regional or city director will have information on how to prepare and participate. You may even want to consider an offering to help sustain the yearly event.

3. If you are planning your own praise parade, consider inviting other nearby congregations to plan and participate.

4. Planning for even the simplest praise parade needs to include these steps.
   - Build a team to pray for and to plan the event.
   - Prewalk the desired route to ascertain the distance and to anticipate problems.
   - Apply for a permit to march through the streets.
   - Secure local police to assist with traffic control.
   - Comply with sound ordinances.
   - Register participants, especially if several churches participate.
   - Rent or borrow trucks with qualified drivers to carry sound equipment to play the music marchers will sing to as they walk.

5. Ask classes, ministry teams, and small groups to make or purchase large banners and to march together.

6. Organizers may want to—
   - provide T-shirts (free or for sale);
   - assign persons to walk the parade route on the sidewalk, offering tracts or fliers to spectators;
   - enlist persons to leave door hangers at each home. Carefully instruct them to stay off lawns.

**Contact or Resource Information**
March for Jesus/Jesus Day. P.O. Box 35976; Richmond, VA 23235; call (804) 745-8400; fax (215) 895-9984; email *info@jesusday.org*; visit *www.jesusday.org*.

## Idea 9: Praise-and-Prayer Celebrations

**Description**
The entire congregation is called together for a focused praise celebration and concentrated prayer. Often, these gatherings may be scheduled around holidays, denominational-emphasis Sundays such as antigambling or domestic-violence awareness, or national initiatives such as March for Jesus.

**Target Audience**
Churchwide

**Implementation Process**
1. Take a long-term look at the church calendar and plan several praise-and-prayer celebrations. Recognize that these events may attract members who do not attend regular prayer meetings. Consider scheduling with events like the following.
   • Sanctity-of-life Sunday—protecting unborn, unsafe babies
   • Martin Luther King, Jr., holiday—racial reconciliation
   • Valentine's Day—asking God for loving churches, families, couples
   • Mother's and Father's Days—blessing families
   • July 4—America's future
   • Back-to-school rally—sending children to school as prayed-over missionaries
   • All Saints' Eve—spiritual warfare for Halloween
   • Prayer for the persecuted church—interceding for persecuted believers
   • Thanksgiving celebration—giving thanks
2. Emphasize a balance of praise and prayer.
   • Singing should be congregational rather than solos.
   • Music should be simple.
   —Assemble a small praise team.
   —Worship leader leads a cappella.
   —Sing along with a worship CD.
   —Begin with a set of praise songs.
   —Return to singing after each prayer segment.
3. Decide on a format.
   • Welcome
   • Congregation stands to greet one another.
   • Praise set
   • Brief teaching to give biblical context to the evening's focus
   • Prayer: emphasize one aspect of the issue or type of prayer (praise).
   —Praise
   —Prayer: emphasize another aspect of the issue or type of prayer (petition).
   —Scripture
   —Prayer: emphasize a different aspect or type of prayer (thanksgiving).
4. Utilize various formats for prayer.

   • *Sequence.* Praising, repenting, asking, yielding
   • *Appointed.* Several pray from the front on an assigned theme.
   • *Small groups.* Leader gives themes to four or five persons in small groups.
   • *Open microphone.* Individuals are invited to lead the congregation from the front.

## Idea 10: Prayer Breakfast

**Description**
The promise of food and fellowship is an excellent way to introduce church members to a more active prayer experience. A prayer-breakfast menu may vary from stand-up continental style to homemade egg casserole served at tables to a catered meal at a marquee hotel. Each serves a different purpose and attracts a different audience.

**Target Audiences**
Men's ministry, women's ministry, community

**Implementation Process**
First let's consider a simple version of the prayer breakfast.
1. Someone agrees to bring doughnuts. Another arrives early to start the coffee.
2. Informal conversation takes place as participants arrive.
3. Participants move to a circle of chairs at a prescribed time.
4. The leader sets the focus, and prayer begins.
   Often, a group of men gathers early, prays for an hour, then leaves for work.

The church-breakfast version requires more preparation time.
1. A team of people agrees to cook a meal, or a caterer is hired.
2. Tickets or reservations are required.
3. The meal is served at tables.
4. Prayer takes place both from the front (have several persons pray on an assigned focus or read Scripture) and at the tables (have participants pray in groups of two or three).
Following a sunrise service, the youth group might choose to serve, sing, and receive offerings. Any other group or class in the church that wants to pro-

mote prayer among its members might also choose this plan.

Another option is the hotel version.

1. Reserve a banquet room at a hotel, selecting the site and the cost of the meal based on your target audience.
2. Plan a program that reflects the prayer level of your audience.
3. At a mayor's prayer breakfast the program should highlight a known musician and speaker, while the prayers should come from the front.
4. A National Day of Prayer breakfast would be conducted the same way, but participants may be encouraged to pray silently at their tables or asked to participate by standing or joining an after-the-program prayer circle near the front. This version is well suited to introducing friends and business associates to nonpolitical prayer with a passionate concern for national morality. All parties and denominations are welcome, but when you gather, gather as citizens praying to the God of all creation.

## Idea 11: Prayer Musical

### Description

A prayer musical presents a call to prayer, repentance, and spiritual awakening throughout the land. A prayer concert is not the same as a concert of prayer. The latter involves the congregation in singing and praying. A prayer concert uses choirs, music groups, soloists, drama teams, Scripture readers, and/or media for praise and worship. The congregation may participate in a variety of ways.

The purposes of a prayer musical are—

* to introduce the congregation to an evening of music that focuses attention on the need for God's people to humble themselves and pray (see 2 Chron. 7:14);
* to develop a closer partnership between the prayer ministry and the worship team;
* to provide a nonthreatening context in which several churches may express their unity in Christ.

### Target Audience
Churchwide

### Implementation Process

1. The prayer coordinator and the worship leader or choir director work together to—
   * agree on the purpose;
   * define the program;
   * incorporate congregational participation;
   * gather a team to execute the plan;
   * support the project in prayer.
2. Select from these program options.
   * Choose a published musical that provides resources for vocalists and musicians.
   * Incorporate Scripture reading and dramatic vignettes.
   * Select familiar hymns and praise that, when presented by a choir or a praise team and interwoven with Scriptures and drama or commentary, present a single theme or message.
   * Organize a combined-church choir that will present the musical.
   * Utilize a variety of choirs, music groups, and soloists.
3. Plan ways to encourage the congregation to participate.
   * Involve the congregation by asking them to sing with the choir or music group when appropriate.
   * Direct them into times of prayer, either silent or with two or three members seated near them.
4. Recruit a team to form task forces to help them get the job done. This will probably double the number of persons who become involved in the prayer concert. Assign persons to communications, media, technical production, set design, graphic arts/concert program cover, and tickets/publicity.
5. Ask prayer groups to pray before, during (on-site prayer during the performance), and after the prayer concert, especially if the congregation will be asked to respond at the conclusion of the performance.

### Contact or Resource Information
*Heal Our Land.* CD or cassette by Wesley Putnam. Selected songs in octavos. Call (800) 530-4949 to order; email *wputnam@wesleyputnam.org*; visit *www.wesleyputnam.org*.

## Idea 12: Prayer Parties

### Description

Prayer parties intentionally combine two aspects of the church we usually keep separate. A prayer party is one hour of praying, beginning with a specific focus and followed by refreshments and fellowship. The hopes are that church members will see this summertime gathering as an opportunity for fellowship at a time of the year when many are scattered and that prayer leaders will create opportunities for more of the congregation to participate in prayer.

The goals of a prayer party are—

• focused prayer for the ministries of your church;
• fellowship that results whenever believers gather;
• opportunities to make new friendships.

Prayer parties do not take prayer lightly but place it in the context of relaxed and informal conversation. If the party is clearly publicized, many who usually avoid prayer meetings may give prayer a chance.

### Target Audience
Churchwide

### Implementation Process
1. Send to prospective leaders of the event a letter that describes the purpose and the process.
2. Determine the location.
3. Promote the party by making phone calls, distributing invitations on Sunday, using a bulletin insert, and posting signs.
4. Ask someone to bring a jug of lemonade and cookies or pie—simple and cool.
5. Begin promptly at 7:00 p.m.
6. Ask participants to introduce themselves and to describe their summer vacations in one or two sentences.
7. Explain the focus of prayer (intercession and petition on behalf of the identified ministry) and the following process.
   • Pray when you are led.
   • Listen to preceding prayers so that everyone moves in a similar direction.
   • Petition on behalf of persons and needs, your church, and all of the redeemed.
   • You may read Scripture as your prayer, begin a song, or ask a question.

8. Stop at 8:00 and invite everyone to stay for 15 to 20 minutes for refreshments.
9. Call and leave your pastor an update the next morning.

## Idea 13: Prayer Retreat

### Description

A prayer retreat is an opportunity to get away for a day or several days to focus on prayer or to pray.

### Target Audiences
Groups of all ages, prayer teams, leadership teams

### Implementation Process
1. Decide on the purpose and details of the retreat.
   • Time spent praying or learning more about praying?
   • Open to anyone or to a specific target group (youth, intercessors, leadership team)?
   • For beginners or for those more experienced?
   • Led by an in-house personality or a guest facilitator or speaker?
   • Will participants pay all costs, or will costs be covered by the church budget?
   • Brief (one day) or long (weekend or weeklong)?
   • Held at church facilities (teaching-focused) or a retreat center (praying, relating)?
   • Will it be led by a worship leader, or will members lead in songs of praise?
   • Will a topic be assigned to a teacher, or will a facilitator teach what he wants?
2. Design a praying retreat.
   • Make certain participants know they will be in several hour-long prayer sessions.
   • Assist participants' preparation.
   —Provide notebooks for preretreat journaling.
   —Suggest preretreat Scripture readings.
   —Give each participant an article or a chapter of a book on prayer to read.
   • Provide a schedule.
   —Friday evening: praise and prayer focused on God's holiness and goodness
   —Saturday morning: praise and prayer focused on confession and repentance
   —Saturday afternoon: praise and prayer focused on our righteousness in Christ

—Saturday evening: praise and prayer celebrating our life together in Christ

• Recognize limitations.

—Beginners may be more willing than able. End sessions before they have been pushed beyond their ability or endurance.

—Children have longer attention spans if they are engaged by the activity, but they need variety, change of focus, and freedom to move.

3. Provide help during the retreat.

• Be ready to make changes necessary to follow the leading of the Holy Spirit.

• Consider coming together for the Lord's Supper.

• Give participants the same portion of Scripture and send them on solo prayerwalks. Debrief by moving directly into prayer on returning.

• Allow time for individuals to be on their own, seek fellowship with others, rest, read, and play.

4. Build on the retreat's success.

• Ask for an opportunity to give a report through an announcement or the church newsletter.

• Share ways people met God on the retreat. This is an effective way to begin promoting the next retreat.

## Idea 14: Prayer Vigil

**Description**

A vigil is a watch kept during normal sleeping hours. A prayer vigil is an all-night or late-night prayer meeting when church leaders bring the congregation together to pray for special guidance or mercy. A crisis in someone's life, in the church, or in the nation is often required before the church gathers for a prayer vigil. In the Chinese alphabet the character for *crisis* conveys two concepts, danger and opportunity. When the church faces danger, serious and concerted prayer will expose the opportunity.

**Target Audience**
Churchwide

**Implementation Process**

1. In an emergency quickly communicate throughout your prayer network.

• Ask for a season of prayer for a designated hour in everyone's home.

• Invite those who are able to gather at the

church, in a home, or at the hospital for several hours of prayer.

2. When you have time to plan—

• place notices in the church bulletin or newsletter;

• make clear the purpose of the vigil;

• indicate whether children are welcome. ("Children and youth who will participate are welcome to come with their parents" or "Sorry, no child care.")

3. Involve as many persons as possible.

• Lead a segment of praise or worship.

• Guide a season of focused prayer.

• Present a brief teaching on an element of prayer or on the issue at hand.

4. Ask the pastor to preach the Sunday before or the morning of the prayer vigil on the need for or the purpose of this prayer vigil.

5. Handle practical details, such as whether to provide juice or light refreshments, the need to lock the door at a certain hour, or the need for late-night parking-lot escorts.

6. The best agenda for the prayer vigil is the Holy Spirit's agenda. Prayer leaders should come prepared with a proposed agenda. However, they should also agree and communicate at the outset that they will seek the Lord's guidance and will change course if He directs. This ensures that you will not try to fit the Spirit into a predetermined format. Here is a suggested way to begin.

• People read a suggested Scripture and yield their hearts to the Lord in prayer as others arrive.

• Welcome and brief explanation of how a prayer vigil works

• A prayer asking God to bring the group into His presence

• Worship

• A season of prayer focused on praise

• Exhortation from the Word

• A season of prayer focused on repentance

—Small groups

—Open-microphone confession

—Praise and worship

—Exhortation from the Word

• A season of prayer focused on asking (petition and intercession)

—Small groups or triads

—Assigned leaders pray from the front to begin new topics

—Praise and worship

—Exhortation from the Word

- A season of prayer focused on yielding to the Holy Spirit through praise and worship

7. Consider exploring other possibilities.

- Send everyone on a prayerwalk throughout the building.
- Ask each participant to find a quiet place to pray and listen. When you return, spend some time sharing what the Lord said.
- Move as one group to various locations to spend a season in focused prayer.

—Focus on worship from the choir loft.

—Repent at the steps to the platform.

—Pray for the nation at a flag.

—Form a circle around the communion table and praise Jesus.

—Touch and pray at each seat.

—Pray for the lost from the porch or outside the front entrance.

- Conclude with breakfast.

## Idea 15: Prayerwalking

### Description

Prayerwalking may be the fastest-growing method God is using in our country to mobilize people to pray. Prayerwalking is praying at the geographical area where you want God to work. Some have called this practice praying on site with insight or moving out of the prayer closet and into the world. Prayerwalkers pray with their eyes open as they walk through a particular area while asking God to do a particular work.

### Target Audience

From youth to adults

### Implementation Process

1. You sense in prayer that God is leading you to pray for something in particular in your world. Examples could be evangelizing your neighborhood, holding a Vacation Bible School, changing the spiritual climate of the local high school, going on a mission trip to a closed country, or a revival week in your church.

2. Promote and recruit church members to prayerwalk for the event or emphasis.

3. Hold one- to two-hour training on the day of the event. Cover the following topics.

- Explain its history. There is no father of the movement. Different people and churches in many locations began doing this simultaneously apart from discussing it with others. It probably began in the 1970s and continued gaining strength until it began to be so widespread by the 1990s that it was given a name. Evidently, God's Spirit began leading people to do it at a grassroots level.
- Teach the need to pray in general.
- Address the specific issues unique to prayerwalking.

—Pray while walking with your eyes open.

—Pray based on what your eyes see. Examples: if you are prayerwalking in the preschool area of your church, pray for things related to toddlers; if you are in the pastor's study and see his study books all over the desk, pray for the sermon. Help participants understand that they may gain insight for later prayers through visual observation.

—Preferably, break into groups of twos and threes. Interaction among prayerwalkers becomes more difficult with greater numbers.

—Have short prayers. Absolutely no monologues!

5. Debrief after the prayerwalk.

- Ask volunteers to share ways the experience affected them.
- Ask them to write down what they asked God to do and to be ready to share when God answers the prayer. This creates watchfulness and expectation.

## Idea 16: Prayerwalking: Christmas Prayerwalk

### Description

Combine the ministry of prayer with the celebration of Christmas. Most unchurched people expect and appreciate caroling, parties, visits, and gifts. A Christmas prayerwalk seeks to take advantage of the community's openness at this time of the year.

**Target Audience**
Churchwide

**Implementation Process**

1. Determine whether this is a churchwide event or a suggested assignment for Sunday School classes, weekday studies, family ministry, small groups, and ministry teams.

2. Begin communicating the vision for the event to appropriate leaders several months before the advent of the Christmas season: "Let's put Christ back into Christmas by bringing Jesus to every home." The effectiveness of this project will be determined more by peer leadership than by up-front promotion.

3. Organize a temporary task force that seeks a prayer-birthed strategy;

4. Order resources early so that sufficient supplies are on hand when needed and so that leaders have ample time to become familiar with their use and benefits.
   - *Jesus* videos
   - Christmas cards
   - Christmas Scripture brochures or tracts
   - New Testaments or Bibles

5. Make a plan: date, start, and stop time; area or location of the prayerwalk; debriefing.

6. Promote the Christmas prayerwalk as an opportunity to pray for and share the good news of Christ with your neighbors.

7. Employ this strategy.
   - Prayerwalk on a certain street, praying for each household as you walk.
   - Select homes of persons known by church members to sing Christmas carols. Or give them *Jesus* videos and encourage parents to show their children the first Christmas. Or hand deliver Christmas cards that share the gospel message along with a gift or a plate of cookies.
   - After caroling, ask for permission to pray for the family's Christmas prayer requests.
   - If personal contacts are made, make certain someone commits to a follow-up phone call, visit, or invitation to the group's next activity.

**Contact or Resource Information**
*Jesus* video. Call (800) 432-1997; fax (949) 492-0381; *www.jesusfilmstore.com.*

# Idea 17: Prayerwalking: Prayerwalk Sunday

**Description**
The entire congregation is mobilized to prayerwalk in the neighborhood surrounding the church facility at the conclusion of a Sunday service. This activity teaches both young and old, new believers and veteran disciples that—
- our church is serious about prayer;
- Christians must get out of their seats and into the streets;
- the church's call is to declare that God reigns and rules everywhere;
- children, youth, and adults are all valuable to the church's ministry.

**Target Audience**
Churchwide

**Implementation Process**

1. Schedule Prayerwalk Sunday at a time when your pastor will agree to preach on the power of praying on site with insight.

2. Your pastor may suggest inviting a guest who has a ministry in the area of prayer or prayerwalking to teach your congregation about prayerwalking and then mobilize and lead them into action. This could provide training for the prayer leaders in your church for future prayerwalks.

3. Prayerwalk Sunday would be best scheduled following a Prayerwalk Weekend that includes these activities.
   - Friday evening: concert of prayer with a focus on the lost
   - Saturday: prayerwalk workshop or seminar
   - Sunday: prayer-evangelism-focused sermon
   - Sunday: prayerwalk immediately following the benediction
   - Sunday: Return to the church for food, fellowship, shared stories, testimonies, and prayer.

4. Determine the most efficient way to send your people into the streets.
   - You can use a parade line, with everyone following the same path.
   - Groups assemble and are free to walk as they sense God's leading but agree to return at a specific time.

- Existing groups are assigned a path but must break into pairs or triads. No more than three can walk, pray, and talk together.
- Pairs or triads pull a destination or an address from a fishbowl and walk there, praying for that household, school, or business center.
- Pray conversationally, as in a normal dialogue; no long or loud prayers are permitted.
- Pray with eyes open.

5. When you send them out, emphasize the following goals.
   - Our desire is to bless others—even our enemies.
   - This is a prayerwalk. Walk. Pray. Talk later. Eat later.
   - We do not want to look or sound "religious."
   - We want to be good neighbors. Stay off lawns. Do not trespass.
   - Be prepared for a divine appointment—an opportunity to explain who we are; what we are doing; why we pray for others; and possibly, an opportunity to pray for that person.
6. When you reassemble, ask these questions.
   - How did the Holy Spirit lead or guide your prayers?
   - What did you see with the natural eye that had spiritual significance?
   - Did the Lord provide any divine appointments?
   - Be certain to include children and youth. Their observations will surprise you!

### Contact or Resource Information

Way Makers. Write to P.O. Box 203131; Austin, TX; 78720-3131; call (800) 264-5214; fax (512) 219-1999; *www.waymakers.org*.

# Idea 18: Prayerwalking: Progressive-Supper Prayerwalk

### Description

Small groups usually meet in the midst of neighborhoods and communities that are overflowing with lost persons. Church members gather in homes that are within a three- or four-minute walk of many neighbors who are either unchurched or unsaved.

What could happen if small groups, including youth, are asked to pray for the neighbors who live near the host family? Progressive-supper prayerwalks are nonthreatening ways to introduce small-group

members to an exciting and effective way of focusing on unbelievers.

### Target Audience

Small groups

### Implementation Process

1. Invite small-group leaders to a brief meeting to introduce the concept. Meet in a home, yours if possible. Promise to spend no more than 30 minutes talking about the idea. Guarantee that they may leave after just 30 exciting minutes of prayer. Have enough umbrellas for participants to use if it is raining.
2. Explain.
   - Christian households have spiritual authority.
   - Our gatherings in these homes, therefore, have a responsibility for the lost.
   - The Holy Spirit is leading His church to pray on site with insight.
   - As we walk on site, we will pray blessings for each home, family, business, and school in sight.
3. Demonstrate.
   - Send out the small-group leaders in pairs.
   - Pray as you walk and observe the neighborhood.
4. Evaluate.
   - Discuss what each pair saw, how they prayed, and what they learned. Agree on a plan to send out every small group in prayer.
   - Prayerwalks can occur at the beginning or conclusion of every small-group meeting.
5. Each small group should then plan a progressive supper, when the entire group travels to several members' homes for each successive course of the meal (appetizer, soup, main course, dessert). At each stop, after sufficient time for eating and fellowship, lead the group to prayerwalk through the host's neighborhood. At the final stop, discuss reactions and ideas for future prayerwalks.

# Idea 19: Solemn Assembly

### Description

A solemn or sacred assembly is a call for corporate confession and repentance. Leaders present the need, which arises from sin in your church or nation, assist church members in preparing for the assembly, and appoint someone to guide the entire church through the cleansing process.

**Target Audience**
Churchwide

**Implementation Process**
1. This project should be the result of a prompting by the Holy Spirit. A solemn assembly should be an assignment from above, not an activity on the calendar.
2. Leaders must clearly communicate that—
   * confession is necessary in the life of a healthy church;
   * holiness is vital to Christian living because it expresses that our lives and church are set apart to and for God;
   * confession is not rules, regulations, and restrictions devised by people to keep us from temptation or sin;
   * confession is not a one-time occurrence but a process;
   * confession requires the Spirit's cleansing, which results from our confession;
   * confession is agreeing with God's view of ourselves and our sin;
   * confession may result in outward evidence but does not require tears or weeping;
   * confession becomes gossip when unnecessary details and names are exposed;
   * repentance is a change of mind that results in a change of direction;
   * repentance is turning from a sin- and self-focused life to a God-focused life.
3. Leaders must prepare the congregation for the solemn assembly. Ask members to come having prepared themselves through prayer. They should not wait for the start of the meeting to begin seeking the Lord. Encourage fasting.
4. Explain practical details such as the length of the service and whether child care will be provided.
5. Follow these instructions to lead a solemn or sacred assembly.
   * Clearly explain how confession will take place: silently at the altar, in small groups, or at an open microphone.
   * Personal or public confession should never be forced or coerced. God may use the solemn assembly to begin a process that will culminate at a later point.
   * The worship leader should select songs and music that draw people into God's presence, sober them to realize His holiness and righteousness, and affirm His grace and forgiveness to those who confess their sin.
   * Select Scriptures that expose sin's true nature and that call God's people to return to Him in faith and obedience.
   * Anticipate a format, but be prepared to change as the Holy Spirit leads.
6. Take these actions after a solemn assembly.
   * Openly speak of how God called the congregation together, prompted confession, and brought cleansing by His Holy Spirit. Church members need to be affirmed that their actions have pleased the Lord.
   * Give God praise for His Spirit-initiated work.
   * Share the hope that is released when God's people obey Him in confession.
   —What has come between us and our God?
   —What are the implications of that sin or distance?
   —What should we do and expect now that we have been forgiven?

**Contact or Resource Information**
International Awakening Ministries. Write to Richard Owen Roberts; International Awakening Ministries; P.O. Box 232; Wheaton, IL 60189-0232; call (630) 653-8616; visit *www.intl-awaken.com.*

# Idea 20: Take-Five Sundays

**Description**
Though valid anytime, a Take-Five Sunday is an especially effective means to introduce a congregation to focused prayer in the midst of the regular worship service. The goal is to take five minutes for prayer in groups of five.

**Target Audience**
Churchwide

**Implementation Process**
1. Determine who will lead the time of prayer (pastor, prayer coordinator, worship leader).

2. Select a focus such as: (1) missionaries, ministries, neighbors, or nations or (2) your church, a sister church, or a not-yet-planted church.

3. Identify in the order of worship or on an overhead screen when the time prayer will begin.

4. Explain the purpose: "Because the Lord calls us to be a house of prayer and God can listen to all of our petitions at once, we'll all join together in praying for the same subject at the same time."

5. Explain the plan: "I invite everyone to stand and gather with four others—no more than five in a cluster, please. If you have never done this before, you may stand in the group and pray silently, or you may simply say, 'Amen' aloud; the Lord will know the prayer of your heart." If children are present, say, "We welcome the participation of children; God listens to simple, sincere prayers."

6. Explain the process: The prayer leader should offer a general prayer asking the Holy Spirit to guide the groups in their specific requests. Then say: "Now each person take a turn praying aloud in your group, three or four sentences, for no more than one minute. You need not go around the circle. Please begin."

7. Consider the following variations.
   • Change the topic or focus by highlighting a new word or photo on an overhead screen.
   • Recruit someone to pray a brief prayer at the beginning of each section. Then allow time for the groups to pray. For example, a member of the congregation prays for their country of origin. Then those in the clusters pray blessings for that nation, followed by someone from another nation.
   • Ask the congregation to stand in their groups with a copy of the bulletin in hand. Then ask each person to select one item from the bulletin (a ministry, segment of the service, name, or need) as the focus of their praise or petition.
   • Invite a ministry team to the front (Sunday School teachers, small-group leaders, mission-team members, deacons, or elders) and ask the congregation to pray for them in groups. Assign prayer-team members to stand with each person at the front, praying for them personally as the groups intercede.

# Idea 21: Week of Prayer

## Description
The entire congregation is mobilized for a concerted focus on prayer for an entire week.

## Target Audience
Churchwide

## Implementation Process
The pastor and the prayer coordinator must work together to implement a week of prayer. The pastor must be burdened to issue this call to the congregation. The prayer coordinator must be willing to handle the administrative and practical details required to mobilize the entire church body for the week of prayer.

1. Design the week of prayer.
   • Purpose: Why do we need concerted prayer?
   • Headline: What phrase captures the vision and communicates our passion?
   • Process: What are we asking our people to do?
   —Pray as a congregation at the church facility?
   —Pray as a family in our homes?
   —Pray in our prayer closets?
   • Guides: What resources could we distribute that would help us reach our goals?

2. Determine the dates for the week of prayer.

3. Share with church leaders both the vision and the need for a week of prayer.

4. Assign church leaders the responsibility of mobilizing their classes, teams, or groups.

5. Help the congregation catch the vision of the week of prayer.
   • Make certain the congregation knows that this is purposeful prayer, not merely another church program they are being asked to support.
   • Use the church bulletin or newsletter and banners to remind everyone of the dates and the purpose.

6. Decide on a format.
   • Seven nights of all-church meetings, asking members to attend any three
   • Seven nights of focused meetings. Choose from these possibilities.
   —A night for youth, families, women, men
   —An evening with other churches in a concert of prayer

—A meeting at a strategic site

—A night for confession and repentance

—A night for praise and celebration

—A preaching-centered meeting

—A no-TV evening, providing resources for family prayer activities

—Friday-night prayer parties, with small groups gathering in homes

—A gathering in homes or at the church building to watch and pray with the nationally televised Concert of Prayer on the National Day of Prayer, the Prayer and Fasting Conference, or a video that leads people to pray

## Idea 22: Workshops, Seminars, Conferences

**Description**

Workshops help a congregation develop a house-of-prayer attitude because members of that congregation organize and implement them. These gatherings not only provide instruction but also bring together persons the Holy Spirit has called to more-than-average prayer. This is often the first step in developing a prayer team in a church. A regular (quarterly) schedule of workshops builds fellowship and relationships among team members. They discover they are not alone while in their prayer closets!

Seminars and conferences allow your prayer-team members to gain a larger vision of the ministry and of the work of prayer. They meet others who have the gift of intercession. They identify with the trials and struggles encountered only by those who are called as late-night watchmen or as intercessors for others' burdens.

**Target Audiences**

Adults, youth

**Implementation Process**

1. Set goals. Consider these.
   • Seventy-five percent of your church attends one prayer workshop each year (may be a video series or a special speaker).
   • Twenty-five percent of your church attends a prayer seminar or conference every two years.
   • Ten percent of your church is trained as intercessors.

2. Create a schedule. Consider this one.
   • Prayer workshop offered once every quarter on Saturday or an evening
   • Prayer seminar offered once every year, possibly a retreat format
   • Prayer conference attended by prayer leader and key intercessors yearly

3. Establish a budget. Include these items.
   • Request scholarship funds for members who cannot pay full registration.
   • Ask for funds to purchase training resources.
   • Submit a request to pay the prayer leader's way to a yearly conference.

4. Decide on a format.
   • Saturday morning
   • Saturday morning and afternoon
   • Friday night, Saturday morning and afternoon
   • Consider using one of the time segments as a laboratory in these prayer activities.
   —Concert of prayer, practicing what has been taught
   —Prayerwalk, taking the principles of prayer into the community
   —Prayer groups meeting in homes to inaugurate a lighthouse of prayer (see idea 33, p. 78).

5. Determine the themes, topics, and teaching that need to be covered this year. Here are some ideas.
   • Developing your personal prayer life
   • Praying your friends to Christ
   • The power of intercession
   • Biblical prayers: our pattern for today

6. Build a team whose members will take assignments for the following.
   • Determining and arranging the most effective location
   • Contacting a guest speaker
   • Providing resources on prayer
   • Producing appropriate publicity
   • Administrating practical details, such as registration, hospitality, and overhead projectors
   • Praise and worship
   • Child care and scholarships for those in need

**PASTOR/LEADERS**

## Idea 23: House-of-Prayer Task Force

### Description
A temporary task force is useful when church leaders are just beginning to realize the need for churchwide prayer or when the congregation's prayer life has become routine.

### Target Audiences
Intercessors, pray-ers with a passion for a prayer-permeated congregation

### Implementation Process
1. With the pastor's permission and full participation, identify the need for a house-of-prayer task force. This task force—
   * does not function like a traditional committee or team;
   * is a short-term, need-meeting, solution-centered team;
   * does not base membership on election or representation;
   * is composed of persons qualified by their gifts, calling, or passion;
   * does not operate on majority rule;
   * is empowered to decide on the basis of what seems good to the task-force members and the Holy Spirit;
   * does not criticize past or present ministry;
   * is future-focused, based on an evaluation of past and present ministry impact.
2. The task force's responsibilities include the following.
   * Provides solutions and ideas that will enable your congregation to become an even greater house of prayer
   * Becomes agents of revival in your congregation, leading to a spiritual awakening in your city and country
   * Provides creative ideas to each ministry team, small group, Sunday School class, Bible study, committee, and team on how to utilize prayer
   * Evaluates the financial and material resources needed for the congregation to be permeated with prayer
   * Makes certain children and youth are not overlooked in the equipping and mobilizing
   * May become a permanent prayer-ministry team dedicated to evaluating, equipping, and mobilizing prayer that transforms people's lives throughout the church
3. The pastor should appoint as the task-force leader someone who demonstrates a passion for prayer and can facilitate meetings and mobilize a small group to communicate the vision to the entire congregation.

## Idea 24: Pastor's Prayer Card

### Description
Each week the pastor sends a "Please pray for me" card to someone in the congregation. This demonstrates the pastor's conviction about the need to pray for one another and serves to involve the entire congregation in prayer for the church.

### Target Audience
Churchwide

### Implementation Process
1. Select your method of communicating.
   * In person by visiting the home
   * Through the mail
   * With a phone call
2. Provide something in print to remind the person how to pray. Choose from these options.
   * Write a letter expressing your thanks and setting a direction for the person's prayers.
   * Produce a postcard that explains what you want the person to do.
   * Purchase greeting cards in which the pastor writes his request for prayer in his own hand.
   * The prayer coordinator or the pastor's office assistant sends out greeting cards. If you choose this option, part of the communication must be a personal word of appreciation or instruction from the pastor.
3. If the pastor knows who is praying for him each week, he can make last-minute contacts to communicate unforeseen needs.
4. The weekly prayer partner should clearly understand how to give feedback. This makes the initiative relational rather than programmatic. It is usu-

ally best if the prayer partners contact the prayer leader rather than the pastor so that the prayer leader can collect or screen the information.

5. Provide prayer-partner support.
   - The pastor should express his gratitude for a congregation who will covenant to pray for him, his sermon preparation, his personal life, and his family life every week.
   - Place a note in the weekly church bulletin or newsletter: "Pray for _____, our pastor's prayer partner this week."

## Idea 25: Pastor's Prayer Partners

### Description
Members of the congregation commit to pray for the pastor and his family.

### Target Audience
Churchwide

### Implementation Process
The pastor determines how, what, when, and with whom he wants to communicate his prayer requests.

1. Choose how and with whom the pastor will communicate.
   - *Open.* Prayer requests are included in the church prayer list.
   - *Volunteer.* Church members volunteer to become prayer partners.
   - *Select team.* The pastor identifies those he would like to participate.
2. Build a structure for communicating.
   - The pastor should communicate with one point person for needs and requests.
   - That point person should pass on relevant responses from those praying.
   - The point person should provide an avenue for feedback from intercessors.
   - A wise and cooperative pastor provides more than requests. Express your hope that he will offer feedback to encourage those praying. Many intercessors enjoy praying over their pastor's daily schedule.
3. Choose the methods of communicating with intercessors.
   - *Prayer requests and answers are included in the church prayer list.*

- Prayer partners sign up for a specific day, time, or area of pastoral ministry.
- Prayer partners meet to pray over the pastor before the Sunday service.
- Prayer partners or team members pray for the pastor during the Sunday service.
- Prayer partners call the church office on their scheduled days for their assignments.
—Pastor's schedule—do not divulge names, simply the nature of the meetings
—Pastor's needs, requests, and goals

4. Maintain confidentiality.
   - The pastor should never be requested to share details that could easily become gossip or temptation for weaker prayer partners.
   - The pastor and prayer leader should discuss levels of responsibility.
   —This request may be expressed to the entire congregation.
   —This need should be shared with the partners/team.
   —This problem/concern may be shared only with those we have both identified as trusted intercessors. They understand and have made a commitment to confidentiality (which includes spouses).

### Contact or Resource Information
*Partners in Prayer: Support and Strengthen Your Pastor and Church Leaders* by John C. Maxwell. Order by calling (888) 993-7847 or by visiting *equiporg.org*.

## Idea 26: Planting New Churches by Prayer

### Description
This initiative focuses prayer on the need to plant new churches to reach new people with the gospel.

### Target Audiences
Churchwide, associations

### Implementation Process
1. Become convinced of the need. A majority of the unchurched population and the unreached generation is not being won in sufficient numbers by the current number of churches. *We must plant more*

churches, new churches, and different churches to reach the multitudes not being influenced.

2. Become convinced that every church can start a church through prayer! Regardless of a congregation's size, history, location, or resources, every church that dedicates itself to praying for the birth of new churches becomes a vital partner in the church-planting movement.

3. Share this vision with your church or associational leaders, asking them to make an unprecedented commitment to develop a prayer strategy for planting new churches.

4. Mobilize your congregation.
   • Provide prayer-strategy materials to your prayer groups.
   • Identify church planters and connect them with prayer partners.
   • Teach church planters the necessity of building a prayer-support team.
   • Ask study groups, Sunday School classes, and small groups to adopt a church planter and his new congregation and community.
   • Ask congregations to adopt a ZIP code and pray for several new churches to begin.

5. Mobilize your association.
   • Bring pastors together to catch the vision and to pray.
   • Provide prayer groups with prayer-strategy materials.
   • Identify church planters and connect them with prayer partners.
   • Teach church planters the necessity of building a prayer-support team.
   • Ask studies, classes, and small groups to adopt a church planter.
   • Ask congregations to adopt a ZIP code and pray for several new churches.

6. Teach and train.
   • Teach the biblical basis of churches planting churches.
   • Teach the necessity of planting prayer-birthed, prayer-based congregations.
   • Train church planters in how to develop a praying congregation.
   • Provide workshops and seminars on prayer evangelism and prayerwalking.

7. Hit the streets.
   • Meet with church planters at the site of their new or anticipated church plant to pray together and prayerwalk in the area.
   • Provide area maps and/or household lists to those committed to prayer.
   • Provide feedback and testimonies to those praying for their encouragement.

## Contact or Resource Information
   • Chicago Metro Baptist Association New-Work Team. Call (708) 293-0400.
   • Church-Planting Group, the North American Mission Board of the Southern Baptist Convention. Write to 4200 North Point Parkway; Alpharetta, GA 30022-4176; call (770) 410-6000; fax (770) 410-6082; visit *www.namb.net*.

# Idea 27: Prayer Summit

## Description
A prayer summit brings together persons in similar roles for an extended time of no-agenda prayer. God speaks and sets the agenda through worship, heart preparation, confession, and listening in prayer. Usually, the results are greater unity among participants, personal renewal, and/or understanding God's direction for future service.

## Target Audiences
Leaders such as pastors, worship leaders, educational ministers, youth ministers, other key leaders or staff

## Implementation Process
1. Consider utilizing the guidance and coordination of International Renewal Ministries. It directs summits around the world for pastors, women in leadership, and citywide leadership teams.
2. If you are planning a summit for your church staff or church-leadership team or for the pastors in your association, consider these factors.
   • *Length*. The prayer summits begins Monday afternoon and concludes Thursday at noon.
   • *Dates*. Plan far enough in advance that this event has priority on everyone's calendar.
   • *Location*. A retreat setting establishes a relaxed, relational, and responsive atmosphere.
   • *Transportation*. The summit works best when all participants travel together in a bus or van(s) so

that they cannot run home or to the office for a few hours.

- *Facilitator.* Someone from outside the assembled group must lead. The facilitator comes from outside the group; the cost to bring in a facilitator is minimal compared to the benefits gained in prayer. The facilitator—

—leads by ensuring that no one other than the Holy Spirit sets the agenda or seeks to control the direction. This requires a delicate balance between listening to God's voice and to the voices in prayer and praise, between discerning when to be silent and when to speak. Strong, assertive leaders can seldom serve in this role.

—selects a listening team of several members from the group, meeting with them before and after each session to gather observations.

3. Seat participants in a circle whenever possible.

4. Often include brief, direction-setting teachings, usually from the facilitator. Although God's Word is essential and foundational, neither teaching nor preaching is incorporated into a summit devoted to intimacy with God.

5. Ask each person to yield to the discipline of praying on focus. Rather than praying one grocery list after another, the group listens for the focus (subject, topic, or direction) of the previous prayer and stays on that focus until released or redirected by the Spirit. When the group is yielded in this way, prayers, songs of praise, and Scriptures read or recited will all converge on a central theme in a true season of prayer.

6. Combine prayers, praise, and Scriptures of praise, thanksgiving, confession, petition, and intercession.

7. Move into a cappella praise whenever a participant spontaneously begins a song or a hymn.

8. Often send participants outside, to their rooms, or on a walk to meditate on the same Scripture section. On returning after at least an hour, participants move directly into prayer, not discussion. God's voice will be heard through the prayers, songs of praise, and Scriptures given in response to the time of meditation.

9. Include neither goal setting nor action planning. Success is measured by spending time in God's presence as you fellowship with one another. Goals and actions usually become evident in the weeks and months that follow. Plan a summit to bless God with the gift of your undivided attention—no strings attached.

**Contact or Resource Information**

International Renewal Ministries. Write to 8435 NE Glisan Street; Portland, OR 97220; call (800) 275-4672; visit *www.multnomah.edu.*

# Idea 28: Pray First; Pray Longer

**Description**

For the church to truly become a house of prayer, each gathering should begin with prayer—but not in the traditional "Let's open with a word of prayer" style. What could happen in your meetings if committee or teams accepted the challenge to pray first and continue until they were finished?

**Target Audiences**

Committees, teams

**Implementation Process**

1. With the pastor's permission write a letter to the head of each appropriate group. Thank them for their service and leadership. Remind them that the church is committed to becoming a house of prayer. Ask permission to address their gathering for five minutes to explain a prayer value the pastor has asked you to instill in every committee and team in the church.

2. Explain to the group that the prayer value is pray first; pray longer. This prayer value simply indicates that we agree to begin every meeting in prayer and to stop only when the Holy Spirit has finished prompting our prayers. We do not pray around the circle or table; each person who is prompted prays.

3. Explain that we pray on target. A new topic is not introduced until the previous issue has been fully prayed for. Usually, several will be prompted to pray about an issue introduced by the first person. After some silence a new need is brought forth, once again with one or more adding petitions. When all are silent, the leader says a simple and quiet Amen to indicate a readiness for business that is prayer-birthed, prayer-bathed, and prayer-based.

4. Send positive reminders to each committee chairperson and team leader. Be willing to model this simple but powerful strategy to release more prayer in more places.

## Idea 29: Praying for Guest Speakers

### Description

Throughout the year your congregation may have several guest speakers. Although most have their own prayer-support teams, it is essential that the host church provide a prayer covering as well.

### Target Audience
Churchwide

### Implementation Process
1. Ask your pastor for as much advance notice as possible about scheduled events or activities that will involve preachers, teachers, musicians, or missionaries from outside your church. Inquire about your pastor's purpose for inviting that particular person. What does he hope the outcome will be for the church body?
2. Seek permission to contact the scheduled speakers to learn their personal and spiritual needs, especially as those needs may relate to their visit with you. When a need or a problem is identified, make certain you know at what level it may be shared: Is this to be kept confidential, or can you share it with the prayer team and/or the congregation?
3. Enlist the entire congregation to pray.
   - Use the church prayer list in the bulletin or newsletter to begin the process of covering the guest and the gathering in prayer.
   - Share a goal and a need, while protecting confidentiality.
   - Distribute an expanded prayer list to teachers and leaders, suggesting that they begin their next class or meeting with a season of prayer for the guest and the meeting.
   - Prayer groups should also receive prayer lists that include requests for the person and the purpose of the event.
   - In the church newsletter suggest that parents devote several evening-meal prayers to the guest's needs. Children could be encouraged to write their prayers or draw pictures,

which could later be given to the guest.
   - Your prayer-advance team should begin petitioning weeks in advance. Their journal entries may be helpful to the visiting minister.
4. Continue to minister on the day of the event.
   - With your pastor's permission arrange hospitality for the guests during their ministry in your church facility. Examples are providing water or juice and ensuring privacy.
   - Ask permission for intercessors to gather around them before they minister to bless them in prayer. They may be more comfortable being seated in the middle of the room than standing while several pray.
   - Express to your guests your team's gratitude for the honor of praying for them during their time of ministry.
   - Ask for permission to inquire throughout the day (if appropriate) for any new needs or requests you could convey to those praying.
5. Warning: A congregation willing to love servants of the Lord in this magnitude will find a long list of prayer assignments! God is looking for houses of prayer that will cover His servants who have inadequate prayer support.

---

**PROGRAMS**

---

## Idea 30: Adoption Prayer

### Description

A prayer group or an entire congregation adopts a focus group of people for prayer. Adopters covenant to pray for a specified length of time and promise to keep confidential what the adopted person shares. By praying for public servants, we demonstrate that God's love and blessings are intended for all persons and that God's people are instruments of blessing.

### Target Audiences
1. *Adopters:* churchwide—individuals, groups, classes, or teams
2. *Adoptees:*
   - Adopt-a-Leader—political community (national or local)
   - Adopt-a-Teacher—education community
   - Adopt-a-School—faculty, administration,

students, athletics (Moms in Touch)
- Adopt-a-Cop—police or fire department
- Adopt-a-Doctor/Dentist/Counselor—medical and health community
- Adopt-a-Hero—entertainment, sports
- Adopt-a-Team—each member of a sports team
- Adopt-a-People—missions (praying for an unreached people group)
- Adopt-a-Nation—missions (leaders and people of that country)
- Adopt-a-Child—orphans (committing monthly support and daily prayer)
- Adopt-a-Gang—spiritual warfare (taking back your community)
- Adopt-a-Street—evangelism (households by name)
- Adopt-a-Pastor—daily prayer for your pastor and his family
- Adopt-a-Church—the health of another congregation
- Adopt-a-Church Plant—for a new work to take root and grow

**Implementation Process**
1. Identify the group God is calling your congregation to support in prayer.
2. Research the focus group.
   - Compile a current list of names of teachers or city-council representatives.
   - Identify current issues or needs.
3. Make contact with the group when possible.
   - Select a point person for the church so that only one person makes prayer requests.
   - Communicate this information.
   —Inform: "Our church has committed to pray for ..."
   —Invite: "I will be your contact person. Give me any needs or requests for yourself or for the group you serve."
4. Communicate with the persons who are praying.
   - Prepare a card or brochure that explains the purpose and power of adopting a group or an individual in prayer.
   - Give the following information.
   —Who they will pray for—by name if possible
   —Why you are supporting this group with prayer (see 1 Tim. 2:1)
   —What their prayer focus should be—how to bless them
   —Where they can post this reminder
   —When they might stop to pray—a suggested time of day
   —How they will receive updates—whether they should contact the person
   - Provide regular updates for the congregation.
5. Set a time limit. Indicate that when the term is complete, adopters are released from their commitments. They may reapply when the adoption process begins again.

**Contact or Resource Information**
- Moms in Touch International. Write to P.O. Box 1120; Poway, CA 92074-1120; call (800) 949-MOMS; visit *www.momsintouch.org.*
- PRAYERPlus Partnership. Write to International Prayer Strategy Office; the International Mission Board of the Southern Baptist Convention; P.O. Box 6767; Richmond, VA 23230-0767; call (888) 462-7729; email *PRAYERplus@imb.org.*

# Idea 31: Family Prayer Altar

**Description**
Each family dedicates a prayer altar for making their home a house of prayer. Many families never pray together, and most merely utter a few words before meals. A family prayer altar encourages more family prayer and greater participation by family members. Even its visible presence is a reminder to pray for one another and to pray without ceasing.

**Target Audience**
Families

**Implementation Process**
1. Coordinate a family-prayer-altar emphasis with every church ministry that relates to the family. Invite each ministry leader or coordinator to an exploratory meeting. Discuss the potential of this emphasis, how each ministry can support the initiative, who will take the lead, and the best time to schedule the emphasis.

2. Begin the emphasis with a message from the pastor on the needs and benefits of a family prayer altar. Make sure members understand that the purpose is to promote prayer among family members and that the items used to make an altar and the placement of the altar are secondary.

3. Provide an information session to recruit, train, and model how a family altar works.

   • Who? Invite the entire family to participate, everyone who lives in the home as well as grandparents or other extended family who would occasionally share in the family's altar.

   • What? Overview the following.

   —Explain a biblical, practical family altar.

   —Give examples of family altars, such as a table centerpiece, a special shelf, or a banner.

   —Gather in families and pray, discuss what to do, and construct.

   —Pray together as a family.

   —Feedback: Discuss what praying together was like, any new ideas family members might have, and your family's commitment to continue praying together.

   • Where? A place where families can work at tables and sit on the floor to pray.

   • When? Whether an evening or a weekend morning, limit the session to 60 or 90 minutes so that family members with short attention spans stay focused.

   • Why? An information session involves every family member, including the father, the younger children, and extended-family members, and allows each person to make creative contributions.

   • How? Instruct participating families to bring materials they may want to use in constructing a family prayer altar, such as craft sticks, material for hanging banners, photographs, and cork board. Leaders should provide materials such as glue, scissors, and markers.

4. To initiate the process, you might want to write and provide for all families a family-prayer-altar guide, asking everyone in the congregation to follow it for the first month. When everyone participates, the entire church prays in agreement—the most powerful kind of petition.

5. Use these ideas to enhance and promote your family-prayer-altar emphasis.

• Post photos of family members who will receive prayer. Change the photos each week.

• Contact persons for requests. Post a list of needs.

• Pray for the church's or denomination's missionaries.

• Post activity announcements to generate prayer for future meetings.

• Encourage family members to write requests and place them on the altar, perhaps in a designated basket. Remind them to read and pray for those requests as they pass the altar.

• A family can invite other families for dinner or snacks and spend time praying at its altar.

## Idea 32: Husband-Wife Prayer Partnerships

**Description**
Most married couples deeply desire a more active and meaningful prayer life. A husband-wife prayer partnership is a covenant that enables the couple to pray together more often and with more satisfaction.

**Target Audiences**
Married couples, engaged couples

**Implementation Process**

1. Gather resources designed to assist married and engaged couples in beginning or resuming a prayer life together.

2. Invite couples to gather in a comfortable setting such as a home to discuss praying as a couple. Give opportunities like the following for couples to take small steps into prayer.

   • Ask a married couple to share their journey of praying together.

   • Facilitate a discussion about the joys and difficulties of praying together.

   • Ask those gathered to share ideas. Each couple must customize their prayer process to meet their own personalities and lifestyle. The main thing is to give priority to prayer.

   • State: "You can pray aloud or silently. When you are finished, simply say, 'Amen.'" Explain that it is OK to start at this point as long as you don't stay there. God hears our hearts, but praying aloud encourages and inspires your partner to continue praying.

3. Explain why praying together is important.

4. Ask each couple first to spend time talking about the following issues before praying together.
   - How do we assess our personal prayer lives?
   - What causes us to pray together—a crisis or a plan?
   - How often do we pray?
   - What would make praying together easier?
   - What covenant do we want to make and for what length of time?

5. Regroup and ask several couples to share parts of their conversation and, if they are willing, their covenants.

6. Discuss these questions.
   - When can we meet again?
   - Will we agree to report on progress?
   - Would you like to be paired with another couple so that you can pray for one another during this commitment? Would you be willing to meet once and pray together as couples?

7. Suggest that engaged couples pray in an environment that would not lend itself to temptation.

## Idea 33: Lighthouses of Prayer

### Description
The congregation is mobilized to pray blessings for their neighborhood, especially their unsaved neighbors, by meeting with others weekly in a lighthouse of prayer. A lighthouse of prayer may be two or more Christians, usually not more than six, gathered in Jesus' name for the purposes of—
- praying: preparing the way of the gospel through intercession;
- caring: demonstrating the gospel by meeting needs with compassion;
- sharing: making the most of every opportunity to present the good news.

### Target Audience
Churchwide

### Implementation Process
1. Adopt the vision to pray for by name and share the gospel in loving and appropriate ways with our families, friends, neighbors, and coworkers.
2. Explain that lighthouses of prayer are small groups of Christians who regularly pray together

specifically for one of these groups.

3. Identify potential lighthouses by listing gatherings such as small groups, Bible studies, men's meetings, and women's meetings.

4. Plan logistics.
   - Lighthouses are asked to meet weekly.
   - Locations must be convenient.
   —Train station before commuting to work
   —School parking lot after dropping off children
   —Parks, gyms, libraries, public facilities, offices
   —Homes where nearby church members may meet to pray
   - The prayer time may be brief. Even 15 minutes of concerted prayer are powerful.

5. Recruit and train lighthouse leaders. You will need a host to provide hospitality and a leader to guide the meeting.
   - Training for prayer:
   —Teach principles and methods of small-group prayer.
   —Provide a workshop on praying your friends to Christ.
   - Training to care: Provide a workshop on ministry or servant evangelism.
   - Training to share: Provide a workshop on *Share Jesus Without Fear, Witnessing Through Your Relationships, Praying Your Friends to Christ,* or FAITH.

6. Promote lighthouses.
   - In every communication piece
   - With a display that includes an opportunity to sign up
   - By praying for lighthouse leaders in a Sunday service
   - With reports and updates as contacts are made with neighbors

7. Keep it simple. Keep it focused. Keep it going.

### Contact or Resource Information
- *Houses of Prayer Everywhere* and *Church Light-house Kit* by Alvin Vander Griend. Call (800) 217-5200; e-mail *info@hopeministries.org;* visit *www.hopeministries.org.*
- *Praying Your Friends to Christ Training Guide, Praying Your Friends to Christ Tract,* and *Taking Prayer to the Streets.* Call (866) 407-NAMB; visit *www.namb.net/catalog.*

- *Share Jesus Without Fear* and FAITH clinics and products. Write to Customer Service Center; One LifeWay Plaza; Nashville, TN 37234-0113; call (800) 458-2772; fax (615) 251-5933; email *customerservice@lifeway.com;* order online at *www.lifeway.com;* or visit a LifeWay Christian Store.

## Idea 34: Prayer Chain/Prayer Network

### Description
One of the oldest and most efficient methods of involving church members in prayer for others is the prayer chain. A prayer chain lists participants in sequence. Each one contacts the next person on the list after having received a prayer request from the preceding person. A prayer-chain captain is usually designated as the first person to receive the request to be passed from person to person.

The chain imagery, though helpful, is being replaced by the term *network*. Consider using the term *prayer network* in conjunction with your church's name. As with a chain, network participants are both receivers and senders, but each sends to several other persons rather than to only one.

### Target Audiences
Churchwide, youth group, Sunday School teachers, ministry teams

### Implementation Process
1. Prayerfully select the prayer-network captain. This person must be—
   - a person who believes in the power of prayer;
   - quickly accessible by phone, fax, or email;
   - responsible to communicate quickly and clearly;
   - willing to be held accountable for the prayer-network team;
   - able to keep shared information confidential;
   - committed to building a team that successfully serves the ministries of the church.
2. Build more than a list.
   - Set expectations high to weed out those more interested in gossip than prayer.
   - Require training (informal, focused conversation on remembering the purpose, roles, and rules).

- Provide a one-page explanation of roles and rules.
- Quarterly the church's prayer leader should bring together the prayer-network team for training, prayer, encouragement, and appreciation.
- Ask the pastor to commission the prayer-network team before the congregation as a sign of its importance to the church's ministry.
- Ask for opportunities to share prayer testimonies of ways the Lord is using the prayer-network team.
- Explain how to initiate a request through the prayer network, such as through the church newsletter or the Sunday order of worship.
- Communicate the qualifications required for persons wanting to join the prayer-network team.
3. Enlarge the focus beyond requests and needs.
   - Thank God. Be careful to search out the answers to previous requests so that you can appreciate what God has done.
   - Praise God. Extol, adore, and praise Him simply for who He is; God need not answer one additional prayer to be worthy of praise.
   - Consider a bulletin-board display with photos of those on the team.
4. Maintain confidentiality. Unless persons have given permission to the prayer-network captain, they should not be identified with their requests. Do not underestimate the temptations and troubles in this area.
5. Consider asking the pastor or another staff member to be the first person contacted by the prayer-network captain when a new request is initiated so that he may act as a filter to eliminate inappropriate requests.
6. Remind team members that God knows the who, what, where, and when of their prayers. He is listening for reasons they are seeking Him and ways they desire Him to respond.

## Idea 35: Prayer-Partner Letters

### Description
Many pastors and missionaries are recruiting prayer-support teams. To make the increased prayer focused and effective, it is vital that the prayed-for leader

communicate with those who support him and his ministry. That communication should include a regular letter to the prayer team.

**Target Audience**
Churchwide

**Implementation Process**
1. Select a contact person for the prayed-for leader so that he or she is not inundated with phone calls and requests.
2. The leader should identify who may receive—
   • general information and requests (usually churchwide for bulletin or newsletter);
   • specific needs (usually limited to those serving on the prayer-partner team);
   • personal issues and concerns of a confidential nature (restricted to a few trusted intercessors).
3. Agree on an unobtrusive manner in which the contact person may seek information.
   • General: by contacting the office or by email
   • Specific: by phone call or email
   • Personal/confidential: one-to-one conversation
4. Agree on how often the pastor or missionary will provide information.
   • General: Leader writes prayer letter that prayer-support team will send.
   • Specific: Leader writes letter or sends email to prayer-support team expressing thanks, needs, short-term schedule, and key goals.
   • Personal/confidential: Leader initiates contact with contact person, especially in case of an emergency.
5. Include in a regular prayer letter—
   • photos, which help those who are visually triggered to pray;
   • brief teachings, which may be saved and used for a future prayer devotional;
   • a brief prayer report from a team member, which shares insights received during prayer;
   • a look back, which motivates pray-ers by letting them know their prayers have had an impact.

## Idea 36: Prayer Triads

**Description**
Three persons, usually of the same gender or age group, commit to pray for three friends or neighbors each and to meet weekly to pray together for those nine persons.

**Target Audiences**
Churchwide, youth

**Implementation Process**
1. Three Christians form a team. Agree on the length of your commitment. Consider praying together for three months.
2. Decide how often you will pray together. Consider three times weekly.
   • Once rotating among your homes or offices
   • Once via a conference phone call
   • Once prayerwalking in one of the neighborhoods
3. Set the length of time you will spend together in prayer. Even 10 minutes of serious, focused prayer can be effective.
4. Share the three names you have committed to pray for, remembering to protect confidentiality. When you are introduced to someone a prayer-triad partner is praying for, be careful what you say or reveal as commonly known information. It is appropriate to say: "I am very glad to meet you, Marcia. Joan has told me about you, and I know that she has been praying for you."
5. Focus on these subjects in your prayers.
   • Obvious needs: physical, emotional, financial
   • Relationships—spouse, children, family, friends
   • Spiritual needs:
   —Softened heart to the Holy Spirit's drawing
   —Open mind to the message of the gospel
   —Awareness of God's presence and work in their lives
   —Favor for you to show and tell God's love
   —Faithfulness to Christ in every word and action
   —Opportunities to care for their real needs through practical acts of kindness
   —Opportunities to share the gospel of Jesus in conversation or through appropriate gifts such as books, tapes, and music
6. Consider asking those on your prayer-triad list for their prayer requests so that you have a reason to talk with them about their lives and ways God is at work on their behalf. They may ask you to pray for others in their families or friendship networks.

**Contact or Resource Information**
- Billy Graham Evangelistic Association. Write to 1 Billy Graham Parkway; Charlotte, NC 28201; call (704) 401-2432; e-mail *info@bgea.org*.
- Love Your Neighbor. Write to 150 Northwest 79th Street; Miami, FL 33150; call (305) 762-7901.
- *An Awesome Way to Pray*. Write to Customer Service Center; One LifeWay Plaza; Nashville, TN 37234-0113; call (800) 458-2772; fax (615) 251-5933; e-mail *customerservice@lifeway.com;* order online at *www.lifeway.com;* or visit a LifeWay Christian Store.

## Idea 37: Senior Saints Prayer Force

**Description**
Aging baby boomers and senior adults are formidable forces to be harnessed for prayer because of their experience, depth, time, and greater understanding of prayer's importance.

**Target Audiences**
Senior adults, retired persons, homebound persons

**Implementation Process**
1. Recognize the valuable contribution seniors can make to your church's prayer ministry. Identify those in this category and invite them to a kickoff meeting that includes food. In larger cities select starting and stopping times that do not coincide with heavy traffic.
2. Follow these steps at the meeting.
   - Affirm senior adults' importance to the church.
   - Prompt them to share stories of the works God has done through the years.
   - Help them connect God's work with His people's prayers.
   - Brainstorm and discuss answers to this question: What could the Lord accomplish if we came together in a covenant of prayer for our congregation, our generation, and our nation?
   - Lead a guided prayer season, first offering prayers of praise to God. End this first season with a hymn of praise. Next, offer prayers of thanksgiving. Spend time allowing the Holy Spirit to convict you of any sin that would limit your effectiveness as a member of this prayer team. Confess as the Holy Spirit leads you. Now you are free and clean to petition God for a birthed-in-prayer strategy as to how to proceed and who should lead. Tell the Lord that you will obey. Conclude with a hymn of dedication.
3. Follow these steps after the meeting.
   - Publicize the formation of the Senior Saints Prayer Force (SSPF) in the church bulletin or newsletter.
   - Commission the members of the SSPF during a worship service.
   - Continually ask how the church can resource or assist them; treat them with dignity.
   - Hold them accountable. They are a vital part of the church's ministry. This is not merely an activity to keep them busy.
   - Include their leaders in the church's leadership-team meetings.
   - Share ideas with SSPF leaders. Ideas may target other seniors, such as prayerwalking in the nursing home, beginning a meals-on-wheels program that includes praying with the recipient of each meal, or turning the next senior-adult trip into a prayer expedition. Or seniors may be recruited to pray for other church ministries, such as missions, evangelism, the pastor, or special events.
4. Don't leave out the homebound. Perhaps a small group of praying seniors could meet at the homes of homebound seniors. Homebound seniors might be connected via phone messages and phone prayer times. They could receive prayer lists and reports. Consider whether team members could escort the homebound to the meetings.

## Idea 38: Visitation Prayer Teams

**Description**
Visitation prayer teams combine home visits with prayers for or with the household receiving the visit.

**Target Audience**
Adults with the gift of mercy, hospitality, or evangelism

**Implementation Process**
1. If you already have a visitation ministry, contact

the director of the visitation ministry and share the idea of incorporating a prayer component into the ministry of visiting Sunday guests.

2. Do not communicate that the visitation ministry is not doing its job or that the prayer leader is trying to take over the visitation ministry.

3. Communicate partnership, cooperation, and an attitude of service.

4. Ask:
   - How can I help you incorporate prayer into the visitation ministry?
   - Do those who visit pray by name for the guests they are going to visit?
   - Are they trained in how to incorporate prayer-walking into visitation?
   - Can we train those involved with visitation in how to ask for prayer requests?
   - Can we train them in how to ask permission to pray before they leave the home?

5. If you do not have a visitation ministry, recruit a team leader who understands the dynamics of prayer evangelism. Together design the components and qualifications for a visitation prayer team. Meet weekly to visit the homes of last Sunday's guests.
   - As phone calls are being made to alert guests of your visit, the remaining team members pray by name for the members of each household.
   - Visiting teams should deliver a gift on behalf of the church, for example, a pie or loaf of bread.
   - Team members are willing to receive training in communication skills and the dynamics of praying for others.

6. Train team members to follow a basic format.
   - Contact the home to alert the family to the team's brief visit. State: "We promise not to take more than 8 to 10 minutes. We truly just want to say hello and leave a small gift with you from our congregation."
   - Be prepared to hold the entire visit at the door if the person does not invite you inside.
   - As the lead person shares that you are glad they came to church, other team members are praying silently for openness, fertile soil, and a willingness to receive prayer.
   - At the conclusion of the visit, based on the Spirit's leading, ask whether they have a prayer request your team can pray for during the week or whether they have a need you can pray about before you leave.
   - Ask whether their request may be included on a prayer list circulated throughout the church.
   - Ask for permission to contact them again to learn how God is responding to these prayers for their needs.
   - Teams that regroup at the church facility can pray over each name and the needs that were shared during the visits.
   - Teams that disperse after their visits should pray together before they drive away from the visited home.

## Idea 39: Wall of Prayer

### Description
Members of the congregation commit to pray during one assigned hour each week. The goal is to have someone praying on behalf of the church and its ministries as many of the 168 hours of the week as possible. This is often called 24/7 (24 hours a day, 7 days a week). When one member finishes praying, he contacts the next intercessor by phone. This idea is based on the watchmen on the walls of Jerusalem who interceded for Israel (see Isa. 62:6-7).

### Target Audience
Churchwide

### Implementation Process
1. Decide whether it is reasonable to anticipate total coverage (24/7) or whether you should focus on specific blocks of time.
   - Cover one full day first.
   - Cover mealtimes.
   - Allow participants to choose from all 168 hours.
   - Ask participants to commit to an entire day, aiming to cover each day of the month. They would not be expected to pray the entire 24 hours of that day but would be given liberty to set their own times and formats.

2. Recruit an artist to prepare a large display that can be visible in the lobby, in the hallway, or at the front of the sanctuary. This will be a regular reminder to the entire congregation and to the individuals who have made commitments.

3. Communicate with those praying.
- Be clear about the length of the commitment, for example, six months or one year.
- Some volunteers will choose to continue and recommit when you start over, but some will need to move on to another task or ministry.
- Not all intercessors will remember their commitments. Recruit someone with the gift of administration to send weekly reminders and to complete monthly reports.
- You may also ask each participant to phone the next in line when the hour of prayer is over.
- The prayer coordinator should send intercessors regular updates with—
—praise reports for giving thanks to God;
—prayer requests for intercession and petition;
—prayer articles. Consider a bulk subscription to *Pray!* magazine.
- Explain several fasting methods so that intercessors can fast at least once during the period of their commitment.
- Consider gathering all 168 intercessors to pray together once during the commitment.

4. Communicate with the congregation.
- Ask church members to pray for the intercessors whenever they look at a clock or their watch.
- At least once during the season of the commitment, ask participants to stand as members of the congregation and pray for the intercessor nearest them. Prayer support for those who support in prayer is a vital secret of spiritual warfare.

## Contact or Resource Information
- *Watchman Prayer Ministry Planning Kit* and *Watchman Prayer Guide*. Write to Customer Service Center; One LifeWay Plaza; Nashville, TN 37234-0113; call (800) 458-2772; fax (615) 251-5933; email *customerservice@lifeway.com;* order online at *www.lifeway.com;* or visit a LifeWay Christian Store.
- *Pray!* magazine. Write to *Pray!* Magazine; NavPress; P.O. Box 35002; Colorado Springs, CO 80935; call (800) 366-7788; fax (800) 343-3902; visit *www.praymag.com.*

---

### PROMOTION/AWARENESS/ PRINTED RESOURCES

# Idea 40: Church-Bulletin Inserts

## Description
Prayer leaders often overlook or undervalue the benefits of their weekly church bulletin to—
- inspire church members by communicating a Great Commission prayer vision;
- inform church members about prayer events, groups, and resources;
- instruct church members through brief teachings or articles;
- invite church members to pray for the church throughout the week.

## Target Audience
Churchwide

## Implementation Process: Church-Bulletin Checkup
1. Devote a section of the bulletin to prayer.
2. Declare your vision at the top of that section.
3. List every prayer group (focus, contact person, phone number, time, location).
4. Have praise (answered prayers) and petitions (names and needs) prayer lists that are updated weekly.
5. Provide a prayer-request and prayer-response form (perforated, if possible) for members to submit their needs and answers.
6. Refer to the prayer list weekly during announcements (if perforated, ask everyone to tear it off during announcements or for a prayer time that follows).
7. Identify prayer workshops, seminars, and conferences.
8. Include a nationally produced insert to inform and inspire at least monthly.
9. Insert reproducible articles on prayer.
10. Provide risk-free-issue cards for prayer magazines and resources.

## Implementation Process: Church-Bulletin Prayer List
1. Quickly identify and use the list (tear-off or perforated panel).
2. List God's answers as well as requests (petitions, intercession).

3. Update weekly (leaving requests from two to five weeks).

4. Include needs of church ministries and missionaries.

5. Have a weekly focus on a neighboring congregation, asking its pastor for his greatest need and the congregation's greatest need.

6. Include requests for new churches in your region or association.

7. Contact youth and children, incorporating their needs and ideas.

**Contact or Resource Information**

Lydia Fellowship International. Write to P.O. Box 15118; Washington, DC 20003; *www.lydiafellowship.org*.

## Idea 41: Church Newsletter

**Description**

Many churches have a regular communication piece sent to the homes of members and attendees. Mailings should always include an item related to prayer. If a regular church newsletter does not exist, a simple prayer letter can be easily produced and mailed.

**Target Audience**
Churchwide

**Implementation Process**

1. Insert a nationally produced prayer guide.

2. Include a reproducible article on an aspect of prayer.

3. Ask a church member to write a brief review on a prayer book or resource.

4. List the church's prayer groups. Include a two- or three-sentence summary from the leader on how God is working in each group.

5. Write a prayer for the entire congregation and ask every reader to pray as they read through the prayer-request section of the newsletter.

6. Present prayer opportunities and activities, explaining how they will equip participants to develop stronger prayer lives and empower your congregation's ministry.

7. Ask your pastor to identify a monthly prayer focus for his life, family, and ministry that can be highlighted in the newsletter.

8. Ask missionaries to communicate their needs (email can speed this process).

9. Use pictures whenever possible (missionaries, groups in prayer, book covers).

10. Provide information for your church members to participate in national initiatives such as National Prayer Accord, Nationally Broadcast Concert of Prayer, and Day of Prayer for the Persecuted Church.

11. Offer risk-free-issue cards for *Pray!* magazine.

12. List Web sites that provide resources and teaching on prayer.

13. In each issue describe a prayer resource for personal prayer, family devotions, or youth- or children-focused devotions.

14. List regional and national prayer workshops, seminars, and conferences.

15. Include a report from the prayer coordinator that reinforces the mission, vision, and purpose of the church's prayer ministry.

**Contact or Resource Information**

- Lydia Fellowship International. P.O. Box 15118; Washington, DC 20003; visit *www.lydiafellowship.org*.

- *Pray!* magazine. Risk-free issues may be ordered by writing to *Pray!* magazine; P.O. Box 35002; Colorado Springs, CO 80935; by calling (719) 531-3555; or visit *www.praymag.com*. Include the number of pieces needed, as well as your event date if that applies.

## Idea 42: Church Prayer Calendars

**Description**

Your congregation can prepare a customized calendar for distribution to every member or household. Church prayer calendars provide constant reminders that your congregation is serious about praying without ceasing and has a faith that believes God for the needs of body, soul, and spirit.

**Target Audience**
Churchwide

**Implementation Process**

1. No computer, typewriter, or photocopy access?
   - Use poster board to make a church calendar.
   - After getting permission, display the calendar on a bulletin board or tape it to a wall.
   - Provide the poster board to a different group, class, or age level monthly and have them choose the daily prayer focus. Encourage creative visual communication.
2. Not quite computerized?
   - Purchase an undated calendar form from an office-supply store.
   - Neatly print a prayer focus for each day.
   - Photocopy and print in the church bulletin or newsletter.
3. Cyberspace technocrat?
   - Use a computer-calendar program to create a monthly calendar.
   - Include a daily prayer focus.
   - Consider giving a related Scripture. When we pray God's Word, we are praying God's will.
   - Calendars may be produced for various age levels or initiatives.
   —Youth, children, families, singles, seniors
   —Praying for our neighborhoods, the nations
4. Use these ideas to expose members to the calendar.
   - Display a poster-sized calendar in the entryway.
   - Produce two monthly calendars, one with church and ministry needs, the second with the names of church members and missionaries on their birthdays and wedding anniversaries.
   - Distribute a family-oriented calendar through the Sunday School or children's ministry.
   - Post an empty calendar at a display area and ask individuals to sign up on the day they or their families will—
   —pray for the church;
   —come to the church building and prayerwalk in the rooms and on the grounds;
   —fast and pray for the daily focus on the prepared church calendar.

## Idea 43: Prayer Central—Display and Resource Center

**Description**

Every church can find a visible and accessible space in which prayer resources can be displayed. This dis-

play is a constant visual reminder of the importance of prayer, a commitment to prayer, and the responsibility to be equipped in more effective prayer.

**Target Audience**

Churchwide, with resources for each age and maturity level

**Implementation Process**

A prayer display or resource center is different from shelving books in the church media library. The church prayer coordinator, with proper permission, can turn even a card-table-sized area into a center of information and action. The display can be an occasional or ongoing emphasis.

1. Customize an inexpensive display board at a quick-print shop. Use slogans like (1) Let's Pray! (2) Stop! Look! Pray! or (3) Prayer Central.
2. Purchase inexpensive plastic displays to hold conference brochures, magazines, and photocopied articles.
3. Ask for funds from the church budget to purchase multiple quantities of a basic prayer guide or pamphlet.
4. Provide low-cost or free items (pamphlets or reproducible articles) for people to look at later.
5. Identify items to be recycled: video training tapes, books, magazines. Attach a label to each resource that reads, "Please return to Prayer Central in two weeks."
6. Offer items for sale. Some bookstores will grant you materials on consignment.
7. Highlight resources that help—
   - parents pray with their children;
   - married couples pray with each other;
   - intercessors.
8. Update your information weekly.
9. Ask for space in the church bulletin or newsletter to mention the latest free article or book to purchase.
10. Consider highlighting your pastor's favorite book on prayer.

**Contact or Resource Information**

Lydia Fellowship International. Write to P.O. Box 15118; Washington, DC 20003; *www.lydiafellowship.org*.

## Idea 44: Prayer Guide

### Description
A prayer guide may be used in a concert of prayer or a solemn assembly, as well as in a special meeting that is not exclusively devoted to prayer.

### Target Audience
Churchwide

### Implementation Process
Use the guide on page 87 as is or as a general guide, selecting your own themes and Scriptures.

## Idea 45: Prayer Reminders

### Description
Everyday items imprinted with prayer sayings or Scriptures may be made available as reminders to pray. Although we must avoid the "Wall Street" approach, reminders can be produced and used in a tasteful and purposeful manner.

### Target Audience
Churchwide

### Implementation Process
1. Discuss your church's policy on the distribution or sale of items such as coffee mugs, pens or pencils, T-shirts, checkbook covers, and key chains.
2. Clearly state the purposes.
   - Reminding church members to pray
   - Inviting community members to call your church for prayer
3. Set the prayer focus.
   - The health and growth of your church
   - Your pastor and staff
   - Your friends and neighbors by name
   - Planting new churches to reach new people
   - Identifying your church as a prayer source for persons with needs
4. Determine guidelines for the merchandise.
   - What items are acceptable?
   - What messages or sayings are appropriate?
   - May we use church logos, phone numbers, and Web sites?
   - Which age groups should participate?
5. Ask hard questions.

- How will we avoid trivializing prayer by turning it into a slogan?
- How will we be certain that those who use the items understand their purpose?
- If we sell the items, how should funds be used?
6. Evaluate.
   - Did we protect the integrity of prayer?
   - Did this project enlist more people in the church's prayer life?
   - Should there be a next time? What should we do similarly? What should be changed?

## Idea 46: Prayer-Sermon Survey— Church Members

### Description
Members of the congregation are asked to respond to a churchwide survey. The pastor will use the results to design a sermon series on prayer.

### Target Audience
Churchwide

### Implementation Process
1. The pastor, church prayer leader, and worship leader agree that this idea will benefit your church in the following ways.
   - Demonstrates leaders' commitment to your church's becoming a house of prayer
   - Engages the entire congregation in thinking about the biblical teachings on prayer
   - Challenges those who pray to develop a greater knowledge of scriptural teachings
   - Encourages those who have weak prayer lives to move deeper into prayer
2. By asking for responses and ideas in the areas of worship and praise, the survey demonstrates that leaders consider prayer an integral part of the entire service.
3. Use the survey on page 88 as is or adapt it to meet your church's needs.

## Idea 47: Prayer-Sermon Survey— Church Neighbors

### Description
Members of the congregation prayerwalk through

## PRAYER GUIDE

Throughout the evening, with eyes to see and ears to hear, offer prayers like the following.

### Praise the Lord

"Lord, we glorify You, for You alone are the Creator and Sustainer of the universe. You are an awesome God—holy, faithful, loving, mighty, and sovereign. We have assembled with the saints to worship You tonight—to declare Your reign and rule over the multitudes who live in our community."

- Our God deserves praise from His people simply because of who He is.
- Tell the Lord we will worship Him; He deserves our obedience and full loyalty.
- Express your love and adoration, your joy at being children of the Most High.

### Give Thanks

"Father in heaven, we are grateful that You have gathered us together—people of different heritage and nations, from different neighborhoods and locations, representing different congregations, born in different generations."

- Give thanks for a gathering of so many different believers.
- Give thanks that God has rescued us from sin through Jesus Christ.
- Give thanks that we are one church of many wonderfully diverse congregations.
- Give thanks for the opportunity and resources God has given you.

### Confess Your Sins

"Make me aware, O Lord, of the sins I have individually committed against You—foolish choices that have broken Your heart, disobedient decisions that have taken me far from Your loving presence. In this moment I confess them to You and ask that, through the forgiveness offered in Christ, You will set my feet once again on the path of righteousness."

- Conviction: a Holy Spirit-initiated awareness of missing the mark God has set
- Confession: to say the same thing God would say about your actions

- Repentance: a change of mind and direction; action required, emotion optional

### Confess Your Sins

"Make us, the entire congregation, aware, O Lord, of our sins. Remind us of how we as a nation have turned away from You, so that we might ask forgiveness. Reveal Your blessings our city or town has forfeited and ways the church is responsible. Convict us of the church's sins we might confess and begin to repent of—pride, self-sufficiency, stubbornness, lack of faith, critical spirits, divisions, and spirits that are lukewarm to the plight of the lost."

- A sick society is a sign of a weak church.
- Judgment must begin with the house of God.

### Bring Your Petitions

"Holy Spirit, enable us to pray without ceasing tonight."

- As songs are sung, pray the lyrics to God.
- As you view the screen, let the images prompt your prayers of intercession.
- As the sermon is preached, respond to the Lord on behalf of us all.

"Holy Spirit, enlist us, all of us, to pray for our lost by name."

- Ask the Lord to release a passion for prayer on His church.
- Ask Jesus to bring more of our pastors into the fellowship of prayer.
- Ask for prayer leaders, prayer groups, and prayer teams for each congregation.

"Holy Spirit, empower us to share the gospel with the lost."

- Ask the Lord to release on every congregation a burden to reach the lost.
- Ask God to call out persons like Saul and Barnabas from each church to plant new churches.
- Ask for a spirit of unity among the pastors in your area.
- Pray against competitiveness, isolation, and territorialism.
- Bless your _____ (street, community, ZIP code) with a curiosity about Christ.
- Pray for other congregations by name, asking God to include them.

## SAMPLE SURVEY—CHURCH MEMBERS

What is your definition of *prayer?*

_____

_____

How would you like to see prayer incorporated into our services?

_____

_____

If you could assign a speaker one topic on prayer, what would the title be?

_____

_____

Read the following list of possible topics. Circle the number that best represents your response if 1 indicates low interest and 5 indicates high interest.

| | |
|---|---|
| Prayer-warrior character study | 1 2 3 4 5 |
| Paul's power-filled prayers | 1 2 3 4 5 |
| ABCs of prayer | 1 2 3 4 5 |
| Spiritual warfare | 1 2 3 4 5 |
| Jesus' prayer life | 1 2 3 4 5 |
| Intercession and the gift of intercession | 1 2 3 4 5 |
| Praying your friends to Christ | 1 2 3 4 5 |
| How to get answers to prayer | 1 2 3 4 5 |
| How to hear God | 1 2 3 4 5 |

List hymns and songs to include that focus on prayer or may be sung as prayers.

_____

_____

_____

the community, stopping at each home to deliver a survey asking for the community's questions about prayer. Each household is invited to a four-week series on ways prayer can benefit daily life.

**Target Audience**
Community

**Implementation Process**
1. Seek the involvement of the entire church: classes, groups, ministries.
2. Use the survey on page 89 or design a similar one that appeals to persons who are unchurched but still believe in prayer.
3. Instruct prayerwalkers to—
   - pray for every home as they approach the door;
   - bless each household with a new openness and interest in prayer;
   - leave a personal note on the door that is not answered: "Hope you'll return your completed survey. You're invited to hear the results the first Sunday of next month in our 10:00 a.m. service. Call [give number] if you have a prayer request";
   - travel in pairs. The partner not asking the survey questions should be instructed to pray that the person being interviewed will allow the team to pray for them before leaving.
4. Conclude: "Thank you for your time and insights. We very strongly believe in prayer and would be honored to pray for you before we leave. May we say a prayer for you? How can we pray on your behalf?" Other possible conclusions:
   - "Would you like information about the sermon series that will be based on the results of this survey?"
   - "Would you like information on what the Bible says about talking with God?"
   - "Our church has Bibles written in everyday language. May we bring you one as a gift from our church—no strings attached?"
   - "Our church is giving away a video of the life of Jesus. It is exciting for children to see Jesus perform His miracles. Could we bring you a free copy?"

**Contact or Resource Information**
*Jesus* video. Call (800) 432-1997; fax (949) 492-0381; *www.jesusfilmstore.com.*

## SAMPLE SURVEY—CHURCH NEIGHBORS

People are interested in prayer more than ever. Surveys show that a vast majority of people pray every day. Our congregation is studying the way prayer works, and we would appreciate your response.

Has prayer been a positive force in your life?
❑ Yes  ❑ No

What does prayer mean to you? _____

_____

What question would you like answered about prayer?

_____

What would be an interesting sermon topic or teaching on prayer?

_____

Read through the list of possible topics below. Circle the number that best represents your response if 1 indicates low interest and 5 indicates high interest.

| | |
|---|---|
| How to get answers to prayer | 1 2 3 4 5 |
| How to hear God | 1 2 3 4 5 |
| How to pray with power | 1 2 3 4 5 |
| ABCs of prayer | 1 2 3 4 5 |
| Spiritual warfare (Satan, evil) | 1 2 3 4 5 |
| Jesus' prayer life | 1 2 3 4 5 |
| Prayer for healing | 1 2 3 4 5 |
| Praying to know Christ better | 1 2 3 4 5 |

## STRATEGIC PRAYING

## Idea 48: Prayer Points

### Description

Members of the congregation, as individuals, families, or groups, pray at the same time but at different, preassigned locations throughout the community. This method may be used to pray against the enemy's strongholds in your area. The National Day of Prayer, the first Thursday in May, is a good time to introduce prayer points to the congregation.

### Target Audience
Churchwide

### Implementation Process
1. Begin with an understanding of the reasons for and cost of spiritual warfare.
2. Gather a team of intercessors who have researched the spiritual history of the area your church ministers to or has been called to claim for Christ.
3. Provide balanced, biblical training on the purpose and power of praying against strongholds as a means of reducing the enemy's influence over lost people. Selecting sites is similar to looking for the pagan high places in the Old Testament. These sites became high places due to the gross or ongoing use of that location for sin. Confronting the darkness is nothing to be feared but requires the armor of God to stand in Christ's victory over Satan's followers.
4. Ask members to register where they will be at a designated time and to commit to stand in that location for an agreed-on length of time and pray.
5. Pray together several times for wisdom in how to stand in Christ's authority and for discernment to know your particular assignment (location and focus). Some may be called to bless, others to plead for God's forgiveness and intervention, and still others to proclaim God's future hope and intentions.
6. Meet together, if possible, and travel to the various locations. Ask someone to take notes of the group's observations in the natural, physical, or spiritual realm. When you arrive, pray with your eyes open in the mighty name of Jesus, not attempting to be conspicuous. Pray aloud but not to draw attention to yourself. If appropriate, suggest that they hold simple signs reading: Today Is the National Day of Prayer, This Is an Official Prayer Point, or Stop and Pray for America.
7. Return for a debriefing and prayer. What did God say? do? reveal?

## Idea 49: Praying with Boldness

### Description

In Scripture boldness characterized great believers. In prayer they often requested boldness, asked other believers to pray that they would have it, and commanded others to be bold. Boldness was the distinguishing mark that caused the Sanhedrin to notice that Peter and John had been with Jesus. New Testament believers exhibited boldness when they testified about the gospel. This simple method encourages and organizes believers to pray for boldness in witnessing.

### Target Audience

Churchwide

### Implementation Process

1. Have volunteers form groups composed of three prayer partners each.
2. Have these groups present themselves in a Sunday-morning worship service during the invitation.
3. Link the groups together this way.
   - Create a list of the groups in a particular order.
   - Give each group the names of its participants, as well as the names of those in the two groups on each side of it.
   - Have each group's participants pray daily for their two partners, as well as for one linking partner—one person from the other two groups.
4. Give to participants the form at the top of the next column as a reminder.
5. Each participant prays for three persons each day and eight persons on Sunday. Each is prayed for at least 26 times each week for boldness.
6. Churches could be similarly linked through pastors, so that a city or a state would link in prayer for boldness in reaching an area with the gospel.
7. Encourage feedback by having each prayer group meet together once a month to pray and report on God's activity in response to the prayers and on the opportunities God has extended to share the gospel. Once a quarter a time of testimony could draw all those together who are praying across the church, with the pastor reporting results from other churches.

### HOLY BOLDNESS

Pray: "Lord, help [name of prayer partner 1], [name of prayer partner 2], and [name of linking partner] boldly speak the gospel today" (see Eph. 6:19-20).

My two prayer partners I pray for each day:
1. _____ 2. _____

My linking partner for Monday: _____
My linking partner for Tuesday: _____
My linking partner for Wednesday: _____
My linking partner for Thursday: _____
My linking partner for Friday: _____
My linking partner for Saturday: _____

On Sunday pray for all eight persons.

### Contact or Resource Information

Baptist State Convention of Michigan. Write to 8420 Runyan Lake Rd.; Fenton, MI 48430; call (810) 714-1907; fax (810) 714-1955.

### MISCELLANEOUS

## Idea 50: All-Church Prayer List

### Description

To commemorate a special occasion, circulate a prayer list throughout the church with requests, needs, or goals submitted by every individual and/or every class and committee. This is an excellent way to promote prayer, either giving thanks to God for many easily forgotten blessings and answers to prayer or beginning a new year or season with faith-filled prayer.

### Target Audience

Churchwide

### Implementation Process

1. The pastor and prayer coordinator must work together to determine and delegate for—
   - purpose and focus;
   - timing (start and stop dates);

- visibility in Sunday services and in the church bulletin or newsletter;
- administration: gathering information, printing, distributing;
- informing and involving key leaders;
- sharing results with the congregation.
2. Every individual in the congregation submits a one-line message. Every committee, ministry team, and group submits a three- to four-line entry.
3. Decide how entries will be submitted.
   - Identify or leave anonymous?
   - Written as a statement (My goal is ...) or a prayer ("Lord, help me ...")?
   - Simply list or provide a line or a box to mark when request has been prayed for?
4. Members may be encouraged to submit certain types of requests for different seasons of the year.
   - *New Year.* Submit your top-priority goal for the next year.
   - *Church anniversary.* Submit your prayer of thanks for your church or your prayer of hope for your church's future.
   - *Fall.* Submit your ministry goals for the next four months.
   - *Easter.* Submit names of people you are praying for and will invite to your Resurrection Day celebration to hear the gospel.
   - *Summer.* Submit a goal for spiritual growth.
   - *New school year.* Submit a request for school.
   - *Thanksgiving.* Submit a prayer of thanks.

## Idea 51: Commissioning Prayer

### Description
In the life of a congregation the Lord leads many individuals, couples, teams, and families into specific roles of service or acts of ministry. It is often appropriate to announce their entry into ministry by presenting them to the congregation and by laying hands on them in prayer, commissioning them into their roles or projects. The purposes of this focused prayer are to—
- send church members on mission with Christ;
- demonstrate to the congregation that they are all to give prayer support to those who serve or are in need;
- release the power of the entire congregation's multiplied blessing.

**Target Audience**
Churchwide

**Implementation Process**
The congregation's prayer coordinator should work with the pastor to anticipate commissioning-prayer opportunities.
1. When a new ministry team is formed, invite the entire team to receive prayer.
2. When a new season of ministry begins, pray over the teachers and leaders.
3. When a mission trip begins for an individual or a short-term team, invite members to face them and pray for them as they stand across the front.
4. When a group is preparing to represent the church as messengers, read Scripture over them before others pray for them.
5. When a family is moving to another area, invite their best friends to bless them with a prayer.
6. When new members have joined the church, invite several leaders and those who introduced them to the church to stand with them as someone prays on their behalf. If several are being welcomed, ask them to stand in different locations throughout the room. Ask the congregation to cluster around them as someone prays for them.
7. When a baby is being dedicated or blessed, invite the church's children to surround them during prayer.
8. When a new school season is about to begin, pray over the children, youth, teachers, and principals.
9. When a school year has ended, ask returning collegians to stand as you pray for them. Bring graduates to the front, ask their next goal, and pray accordingly.
10. When an individual is scheduled for or has returned from a hospital stay, have the person stand, if possible, as the congregation extends a hand in that direction and someone leads in prayer for healing or thanksgiving.

## Idea 52: Fishbowl of Prayers

### Description
To remind us that we are called to share the gospel with the lost, Jesus told us that we are to think of ourselves as fishers of persons. Our Lord wants us to

witness to those who have not received eternal life. By prominently displaying a fishbowl, you can remind your congregation or your class of our Lord's command to evangelize. Members are encouraged to write on cards the names of the unsaved friends and neighbors they are praying for and to place the cards in the fishbowl. Seeing the fishbowl every week reminds them to pray.

**Target Audience**
Churchwide

**Implementation Process**
1. Purchase a large plastic fishbowl from a pet-supply store. Place a sign on the inside facing the front or alongside the display that explains the purpose and process of praying. Make two identical lists of prayer requests. Drop one in the bowl and post the other at home.
2. Explain that our faith is not in putting a list in a fishbowl. This is a simple action designed to solidify our commitment as a congregation or class to pray earnestly for those we know without Christ.
3. Communicate high expectations of what God does when His people pray. Make the fishbowl display and the cards for the prayer lists high quality. Select an appropriate Scripture verse. Provide clear instructions.
4. Consider using ideas like the following in the bulletin or newsletter to create curiosity.
   • Have you seen the fishbowl?
   • Gone fishin' lately?
   • Who do you know who belongs in the fishbowl?
5. Provide prayer-list forms to all members by mail or by placing them in the church bulletin, asking them to begin praying about who should be on their lists.
6. Focus attention on the fishbowl the first time it is displayed.
   • Hold it before the entire congregation.
   • Ask members to take out the lists they received in the mail or have in their bulletin.
   • Ask them to write several names on it.
   • Place your list in the fishbowl and pray on behalf of the entire group.
   • Consider passing the fishbowl around, asking participants to place their lists in the fishbowl and pray silent, brief prayers of commitment.

• Display the fishbowl in a prominent location. One church has it at the front so that everyone sees it each Sunday.
• Frequently ask for prayer testimonies of ways God is answering prayer.
• Remind your people that we are not merely praying; we also need to take these actions.
—Pray: Ask God to soften hearts and open minds.
—Care: Seek opportunities to demonstrate Christian kindness.
—Share: Witness to someone who needs to hear the good news of Jesus Christ.
—Recycle: After seven or eight weeks, pray for all persons listed. Remove the lists and start the process again to allow participants to pray and care for current needs.

# Idea 53: Offertory Prayer

**Description**
The Sunday offering provides a pastor or prayer leader a wonderful opportunity to introduce fresh prayers that remind the congregation of the purpose of both the offering and the prayer. This emphasis also encourages members' involvement.

**Target Audience**
Churchwide

**Implementation Process**
1. Get your pastor's permission to schedule a variety of persons to lead the prayer for the Sunday offering. Indicate that your goal is to—
   • involve more people in leading the congregation in prayer;
   • refresh what for many may have become a thoughtless moment in the service;
   • engage the entire congregation in praying for and giving their gifts.
2. Consider or reformat these ideas to fit your situation.
   • Ask the congregation to stand during the prayer.
   • Sing or recite the Doxology as the prayer.
   • Invite one who is collecting the offering to lead the prayer.

- Arrange with the worship leader to have a song of praise as the prayer.
- Bring the children to the front and have them hold a gift basket as one of their teachers leads the prayer.
- Ask a child or a youth to say a prayer of thanks to the Lord.
- Lead the congregation in a responsive reading as a means of thanking God before the offering is collected.
- Pray for the gifts after they are collected.
- Place the collection plate or basket at the front and invite the congregation to bring their gifts at any time during the worship section of the service.
- Place the collection plate or basket at the back and remind the congregation to give their offerings as they leave.
- Have a family stand together before the church as one or several family members pray.
- As gifts are collected, use an overhead screen to show pictures and photos of how the offering will be used. You may want to select a different focus each week for several weeks, such as missionaries, staff, ministries, administration, or facilities.
- Ask the congregation to scan the bulletin and to choose a ministry, a staff person, a missionary, an activity, or an event. As tithes and offerings are being collected, ask people to pray silently that God will bless others through your gifts.
- Inform the congregation that two baskets or plates will pass, the first for them to put something in, the second for them to take something out. In the second basket place cards that contain prayer requests. Say, This week give God your gift of prayer by praying for _____.
- Invite the congregation to pray silently over the church prayer list as the offering is collected.

## Idea 54: Prayer Banners

**Description**
Several large banners are hung or displayed at various places in the worship center. Each banner uses words and symbols to depict a focus for prayer.

**Target Audience**
Churchwide

**Implementation Process**
Prayer banners may be placed in the sanctuary to remind the entire congregation, but age-appropriate sets may be placed in rooms where youth and children gather for teaching and fellowship.

Prayer leaders must choose between purchasing premade banners and enlisting skilled persons in the congregation to make banners. Premade banners are usually quickly available and allow leaders to select those that will suit the congregation. Homemade banners utilize members' gifts and allow leaders to choose Scriptures, images, or themes.

Banners become prayer banners when they are used as part of the prayer meeting.

1. Select the major themes of prayer the Lord has assigned your congregation. For example:
   - *Missions.* Pray for the nations to come to Christ.
   - *Children.* Intercede for those unborn and those unsafe.
   - *Church planting.* Pray that God will use your church to start new congregations so that more persons find Christ.
   - *Revival.* Plead for revival in the church that leads to spiritual awakening in our land.
   - *Youth.* Intercede for schools and gangs, asking God to call forth young Christian men and women into leadership.
   - *Prayer.* Pray that the church will become a house of prayer.
   - *Reconciliation.* Pray that believers will be one, showing that God loves the world.
   - *Worship.* Pray that the church will serve God first in authentic praise and adoration.
   - *Love.* Pray that God will empower you to be a "Love one another" church.
   - *Healing.* Pray by name for persons needing physical or emotional health.
   - *Compassion.* Pray for compassion to share resources with those in need.
   - *The lost.* Pray by name for persons whose hearts need to be softened.
2. Break into groups based on the number of banners displayed.
3. Ask each group to stand before a banner and to

pray until you signal them to move to the next banner.

4. Consider signaling the groups with music each time they are to move.

## Idea 55: Prayer Chair

### Description
In a prayer gathering a person voluntarily sits on a chair in the center of the group to receive focused prayer for a need, problem, or upcoming challenge.

### Target Audience
Churchwide

### Implementation Process
This method is appropriate in any group meeting, as long as the person being prayed for is willing and does not feel uncomfortable.

If the request to pray or the request for prayer is a spontaneous response to the prompting of the Holy Spirit after a service or in a large gathering, follow these steps.

1. Form a circle around the person and begin to pray.
2. Move into a less conspicuous setting or into a more private room.
3. Provide a chair, especially if the person is weak or ill.

If the request to pray or the request for prayer occurs in a small group or prayer group, follow these steps.

1. Place a chair in the middle of the circle.
2. Ask the person to share briefly (from one to three minutes) why he is seeking prayer.
3. Invite several from the group to kneel beside the person and to pray aloud while group members pray silently.

During prayer follow these steps.

1. The group leader is an advocate for the subject of prayer.
   • Is the person willing?
   • Is he comfortable so that he may receive the blessings of prayer?
   • Are pray-ers staying focused and praying appropriately?

2. The group leader should listen for the Holy Spirit's leading but must also look for signs that the prayed-for individual is responding.
   • Tears or crying?
   • Facial or physical movement?
   • Peace or anxiety?

3. The group leader, at any time but certainly at the conclusion of the prayers, should ask the prayed-for person how he or she feels, whether God has revealed anything, and whether he has questions or concerns. Comments may be useful in knowing what to pray for or against.

4. The group leader must be sensitive to space and touching issues. Some people need more spatial distance than others; guard those receiving prayer. Some pray-ers want to lay a hand on the person they are praying for without asking permission; intercede if necessary. Also, men should be careful about touching women, especially those who have been victimized. It may be better to ask a female in the group to place a hand on a woman who has a male praying over her. Men should never place a hand over a woman's heart; the woman can do that herself as the man prays for her. The enemy can use both legalism and liberty to detract from the true purpose of prayer.

At prayer summits or in ongoing groups follow these steps.

1. Give participants time to prepare. As the Holy Spirit leads, say, At our next session/meeting a chair will be placed in the center of the circle for anyone led to share a need or to confess a sin.
2. Pray for several persons during a session or meeting.
3. Practice wise and discerning leadership in biblical confession.
4. Do not allow the sharing of details of a sin. Detailed explanations, especially sexual in nature, are never necessary. If someone begins to share inappropriately, the group leader must gently but quickly interrupt and redirect. Everyone, including the one confessing, will be appreciative.

## Idea 56: Prayer-Poster Campaign

### Description
Each youth and children's class is asked to submit

posters that emphasize an aspect of prayer. The posters are displayed throughout the church as reminders of the privilege and power of prayer.

**Target Audience**
Churchwide

**Implementation Process**
1. Coordinate with the youth and children's leaders to make sure they appreciate the campaign and will actively support it.
2. Ask your pastor for optimal scheduling, whether he would like to suggest a theme, and whether the campaign can coincide with a preaching series.
3. Use themes like the following.
   • Pray Without Ceasing
   • More than We Dare Ask or Think
   • Teach Us to Pray
   • Could You Not Watch with Me for One Hour?
   • Prayer Warriors of the Bible
   • Prayer Is _____
   • Stop! Look! Pray!
   • Graffiti prayers. Attach a marker and ask passersby to write prayers based on the focus of that particular poster, such as our neighbors, our nation, our schools, or our ministries.
4. Purchase a sufficient quantity of poster board and make it available at Prayer Central (see idea 43, p. 85).
5. Consider having all participants bring their posters on the same day so that the pastor or the prayer leader can invite them to explain their posters. You may want to stop several times and lead the congregation in prayer. Or ask participants to scatter themselves throughout the room. Then instruct adults to gather around each poster, making certain no poster is omitted, and pray aloud until the worship leader leads the congregation in a song of praise.
6. Provide tape so that each poster can be displayed throughout the worship center, in hallways, in various classrooms, or in the entryway.

## Idea 57: Prayer Recipe Book

**Description**
Members submit prayer recipes for those who hunger and thirst for righteousness, especially when

they encounter trials, troubles, and tribulation. The recipes are then compiled and published as a book.

**Target Audience**
Churchwide

**Implementation Process**
1. Each entry in the book should follow a basic format.
   • A prayer recipe for _____
   • Submitted by _____
   • Scriptural support: a verse or portion that may be prayed back to God as an ingredient in the recipe of spiritual success
   • Brief comments, poetry, testimony, or quotation by the person making the entry
   • Brief prayer

---

**SAMPLE PRAYER RECIPE**

**A Prayer Recipe for Confusion**

Submitted by Phil Miglioratti

"Trust in the Lord with all your heart and lean not on your own understanding; in all your ways acknowledge him, and he will make your paths straight" (Prov. 3:5-6, NIV).

This has become my life verse. It is like a compass when I get confused or am not certain how to make in a decision.

"Thank You, Lord, for wanting us to trust You and to place our hope in You. I know for certain that when I am confused, You know for certain which way to go."

---

2. A prayer recipe book may be printed and distributed by the church or may be adapted by a company that produces traditional church cookbooks.
3. Distribute and sell the book throughout the congregation.
4. Consider the following possibilities for your congregation's prayer recipe book.

- Include several formatted pages for "My Prayer Recipe for _____."
- Include a page titled "My Prayer Request," informing readers that your church would be glad to receive their requests and to pray for their needs.
- Ask for contributions to be used in the church's prayer ministry.
- Print twice as many copies as you anticipate selling. Then give copies to all members who contribute, asking them to give them to neighbors or friends.
- Print enough copies for the neighbors in the community of the church facility and give them away on Prayerwalk Sunday (see idea 17, p. 66).
- Combine efforts with several other churches so that the final product includes entries from a wider variety of people and backgrounds. This could be an excellent way to begin a cooperative relationship with a congregation from a different neighborhood, socioeconomic class, ethnic origin, or denomination.

## Idea 58: Prayer Testimonies

### Description
A prayer testimony shares God's work in a person's life and the significant role of prayer in that work. The testimony combines the power of a personal witness with the crucial lesson of how God works in and through the prayers of His people. This idea can be implemented during worship services, Sunday School classes, Bible studies, and other meetings.

### Target Audience
Churchwide

### Implementation Process
1. Contact persons who have seen victory in their lives, have had answers to prayers for themselves or others, or have submitted prayer requests.
2. Explain to them the way God will use the sharing of their stories to inspire many others in the congregation to deeper faith and more prayer.
3. Offer to interview, asking open-ended questions, individuals who have testimonies but may be uncomfortable speaking in public.
4. Request that those who share prayer testimonies

also include Scriptures, possibly on the benefits or promises of prayer, that have sustained them.
5. After the prayer testimony the leader may—
   - pray while standing beside the person, giving thanks to God and blessing the person who gave the testimony;
   - lead the congregation or class in a song of praise and affirmation;
   - invite the congregation to stand and silently pray for their needs;
   - say, "Let's praise the Lord!" and begin applauding.

## Idea 59: Prayer Tithing

### Description
To permeate the congregation with prayer, every person, family, class, committee, group, and team is asked to give a tenth of their time to prayer, usually for a specified period of time.

### Target Audience
Churchwide

### Implementation Process
1. Coordinate with your pastor a period of time (week or month) when prayer tithing could be the priority focus of the entire congregation.
2. Ensure that the leaders of all classes, committees, groups, and teams build their ownership in the purpose and the process. Their understanding and partnership are vital to ensuring that church members' participation is spiritual rather than programmatic.
3. Be clear about what you are asking.
   - When does this begin, and when does it conclude?
   - Who will be involved?
   - How will church leaders participate?
   - What is the purpose of this tithing time to pray?
   - How will our church benefit?
   - How will each class or group benefit?
   - How can individuals and families participate?
   - Why is this a God-idea and not merely a good idea?
4. Communicate the biblical basis of this idea.
   - The word *tithe* means *one-tenth*. Scripture

records that tithers set aside the first 10 percent of their harvest or earnings. Tithing is an act of obedience indicating faith and dependence on God and gratitude for God's blessings and daily care.

- Those of us who do not plant and harvest the land need to apply the principle and promise of tithing to other areas of our lives—to prayer, for example.
—Groups and committees devote to prayer at least the first 10 percent of their meeting time.
—Individuals and families devote to prayer 10 percent of their evening or their TV time.
- Tithing is not meant to be a legalistic taskmaster. Use prayer tithing—
—to introduce priority prayer into task-focused groups, which are usually led by persons gifted in administration or leadership and may not feel confident in deeper areas of prayer;
—to place more than token prayer in every aspect of church life: home, Sunday School, choir, committee meetings, staff meetings, and small groups.

## Idea 60: Praying for Services

### Description
Many famous preachers had prayer teams that prayed before and during the service to ensure that it was birthed and bathed in prayer. A prayer team offers support before the meeting, during the worship and preaching, and after the service as people respond to the invitation to salvation and confession.

### Target Audience
Trained intercessors

### Implementation Process
1. Ask your pastor's permission and wisdom. Too many God-initiated ideas fail because of a weak or nonexistent partnership between the pastor and prayer leader. Intercessors, valuable assets to their pastor, must respect pastoral authority and be patient for God's timing.
2. Before recruiting a prayer-advance team, take the following steps.
   - Determine the before, during, and after locations.
     —*Before.* In a room that will not be utilized until the service begins or in the sanctuary if pray-ers are free to prayerwalk in the sanctuary/worship center. Prayerwalking is possible even if a choir or praise band is rehearsing.
     —*During.* In a room adjacent to or behind the altar or platform. Some teams have even stationed themselves under the platform. If no rooms or quiet corners are available, a team may sit in the congregation, knowing that intercession is its primary assignment.
     —*After.* A prayer-advance team may sit in the front row to pray for the disbursing congregation, especially those who responded to an invitation, or it may move into the room when it is empty.
   - Discuss qualifications. A prayer-advance team requires mature pray-ers. Qualifications include weekly prayer-group attendance and completion of required training through courses, videos, and workshops.
   - Seek wide support from church leaders. Talk with as many committees, teams, and classes as possible.
   - Inform and educate the congregation so that they appreciate the team's ministry and understand how to become involved.
3. Consider enlisting the following groups to pray.
   - Before—church leaders, ministry leaders, and teachers (scheduled monthly)
   - During—assigned and trained intercessor teams
   - After—assigned and trained prayer team:
     —Intercession for all who have heard the Word of the Lord
     —Petition for those responding to an invitation
     —Hands-on ministry for persons who are suffering or sick
4. Provide a journal in which the leader writes the focus of that day's prayers and Scriptures given by the Holy Spirit during prayer. The leader should hand the journal to the pastor or the church prayer coordinator each week to protect confidentiality. It should not be left out for public viewing.

## Idea 61: Praying the Church Directory

### Description
The goal is to provide prayer support for every per-

son in the congregation by enlisting every person to pray for another church member.

**Target Audience**
Churchwide

**Implementation Process**
1. The effect of this project partially depends on the accuracy of the church directory. Coordinating this project with the church office will give them time and possibly the motivation to update the church directory. Another option is to enlist several callers to make a phone contact with everyone in the church directory, asking for updated information and previewing the new project. Share new information with the church office. Be certain to contact recent guests and new attendees, both to ensure they will be prayed for and to give them another warm touch from your church. This may help them feel more a part of the church family.
2. Use churchwide communication in the form of announcements and the church bulletin or newsletter, especially in a large congregation, to ask for name, address, and phone information.
3. Ask your pastor to write an inspirational letter to include in a mailing.
4. Include a letter from the prayer coordinator explaining what you are asking members to do.
5. Provide the name of one person from the congregation on a card or form. Ask members to—
   • pray for the person assigned to them at least once every day for the next 21 days;
   • contact them once to let them know that someone is praying for them;
   • contact them more often to get specific prayer requests and to pray for them over the phone.
   • share about their experience at a prayer gathering. They should talk not about the person they prayed for but about the way it felt to give prayer support and how God spoke to them as they were praying for someone else.

## Idea 62: Praying the Newspaper

**Description**
A great preacher once said that we should all have a Bible in one hand and a newspaper in the other to help us connect our spiritual concerns with the world's needs. Scanning the local newspaper for concerns to bring to a prayer gathering or group enables participants to intercede for community needs.

**Target Audiences**
Individuals, families, classes or groups, workshops, prayer meetings

**Implementation Process**
Follow this process for individuals.
1. Purchase multiple copies of your local newspaper for persons you have identified as primarily home-based intercessors.
2. Write a cover letter reminding them of your church's desire to pray for the community and the power of intercession.
3. Explain that you are providing the same materials to others, who become a home-based prayer force that prays for the same needs on the same day.
4. Let them know that you welcome their feedback.

Use this process to involve families.
1. Send a letter to parents that explains the purpose and power of praying for others. Provide several Scripture references that parents can use to introduce this at-home activity to their families.
2. Each family member can select a favorite section of the newspaper. A dad or a mom might pray for a local company in the business section or for a national figure identified on the front page. A teenager can pray for an entertainer or a sports hero. Children can find photos they understand and can pray for. Encourage family members to send "We Prayed for You" notes. Articles and photos can be cut from the newspaper and hung on a family-made "We Prayed For" poster.

Classes, groups, workshops, and prayer meetings can follow this process.
1. If possible, ask participants ahead of time to bring newspapers or newsmagazines. Explain the purpose and power of praying for others. Emphasize their role as pray-ers, intercessors, or a prayer team to pray for your community.
2. Begin with a season of yielding prayer, allowing the Holy Spirit to fill (control) participants so that they are led to precise articles, photos, or items.

- *Full group.* Ask pray-ers to stand and pray one at a time. Explain that the Holy Spirit may lead several others to pray for the same situation; do not begin a new topic until the prayers for that need have ceased.
- *Small groups.* Pray-ers need not stand, but give the same instruction not to change the subject until others have had an opportunity to agree with the first person in prayer. Agreement in prayer is a powerful weapon. Or distribute the newspaper page by page to each participant, asking each to highlight one item on the page. Post the pages around the room. Break into several small groups, sending each to a different posting. Give the groups five minutes at each site to pray for the situation or the person. Then ask them to walk to another page.

## Idea 63: Praying the Telephone Directory

### Description
To pray for every household in your community, assign one page of your local telephone directory to each member of your congregation.

### Target Audiences
Churchwide, combined churches

### Implementation Process
1. Determine the following.
   - The territory the Lord is assigning your congregation to cover with prayer.
   - The length of time participants will be asked to commit to prayer.
   - The approximate number of households each participant will receive.
   - How many households per day should be covered (for example, one at each meal would cover three).
2. Consider using this activity as an opportunity to pray together with other congregations.
   - Your pastor should contact other pastors.
   - They could be invited to a brief gathering in which your pastor shares the vision, invites them to be partners, and spends one-third of the time with them in prayer.
   - A combined church concert of prayer could kick

off prayer for every person listed in the phone directory.
3. Children and youth may be included. Give them their own lists for prayer or encourage them to pray for the child or youth in each household.
4. Instruct members to pray evangelistically. Prayer evangelism is—
   - asking that each member of the household will be saved;
   - reminding the Lord that He is unwilling that any should perish (see 2 Pet. 3:9);
   - imploring the Holy Spirit to soften their hearts and to change resistant attitudes;
   - breaking Satan's stronghold and bondage over their lives (see 2 Cor. 10:5);
   - asking God to grant them faith and send believers to them with the gospel;
   - asking the Lord for wisdom to know how to deliver the message of Jesus to them.
5. Consider providing participants "Our Church Prayed for You Today" cards they would send to households on the days they were prayed for.
6. Ask those who pray to send a letter from the pastor that—
   - invites them to church;
   - offers a free *Jesus* video or an easy-to-understand Bible;
   - identifies a phone number they can call to leave a specific prayer request.

### Contact or Resource Information
*Jesus* video. Call (800) 432-1997; fax (949) 492-0381; *www.jesusfilmstore.com.*.

CHAPTER

6

# *Your* SOUTHERN BAPTIST PRAYER CONNECTIONS

## JOHN FRANKLIN

### Vision Statement for Prayer

The Prayer-Strategy Office serves Southern Baptists and their missionaries through a full spectrum of prayer channels and services, thus enabling them to become informed, involved, empowered intercessors that Christ's kingdom may come among all peoples of the earth.

### Prayer Networks

#### CompassionNet

CompassionNet is a computer-based prayer network that is updated daily, Monday through Friday. It features current prayer items for countries, mega-cities, and people groups where Southern Baptists have assigned personnel. It is located on the Internet at *www.imb.org*. E-mail CompassionNet at *prayeroffice@imb.org/compassionnet*.

#### PrayerLine

PrayerLine provides current prayer needs from around the world 24 hours a day on a toll-free telephone line. It also serves as a worldwide urgent-prayer network. The message is changed each Monday, Wednesday, and Friday and in urgent situations. Call (800) 395-PRAY.

#### Global PrayerGram

Global PrayerGram is an effective way to systematically intercede for world missions. The printed guide provides day-by-day strategic requests and developments from all areas of the world where Southern Baptist missionaries serve. For a free subscription call (800) 999-3113.

#### Urgent-Prayer Network

Urgent-Prayer Network enables intercessors to be involved in direct world-missions prayer. It e-mails concise, ready-to-use prayer requests of an urgent nature as these needs arise. E-mail CompassionNet at *prayeroffice@imb.org/compassionnet*.

## Prayer Projects

### Last Frontier Prayer Guide

In nearly every part of the world, groups of people remain who are still untouched by the gospel. Many of them live in areas where access is restricted by resistant governments or religions. More than one thousand Southern Baptist churches are part of a prayer project to pull down those barriers. The IMB offers Last Frontier Collector's Card Set which includes facts, pictures, and prayer needs for multiple people groups. Many people groups have been opened to the gospel as a result of this focused prayer effort. For more information about Last Frontier Collector's Card Set, call (800) 999-3113.

### PRAYERplus Partnership

Southern Baptists have identified more than two thousand unreached people groups that make up the Last Frontier of world evangelization. Churches can enter a partnership with one of the Last Frontier people groups. A church commits to pray without ceasing for the opening and evangelizing of their unreached people group, plus obedience to God in what He directs them to do in coordinated effort with the International Mission Board to evangelize their group. Call (888) 462-7729 or e-mail *prayerplus@imb.org.*

### Prayerwalking

Prayerwalking is literally praying on site with insight. God is calling intercessors to go on prayer journeys to the world's teeming megacities as well as to some of the earth's darkest and most remote areas. For more information call (800) 866-3621.

## Web Site

*www.imb.org* offers links to the projects you have read about, in addition to prayer requests for missions.

**LIFEWAY CHRISTIAN RESOURCES**

## Vision Statement for Prayer

Our purpose is to help churches disciple members in prayer by providing high-quality resources and training.

## Resources

### Youth

- *An Awesome Way to Pray* by Barry St. Clair mobilizes youth prayer teams of three students each to pray three times a week for three lost friends. *Student Journal,* item 0-7673-9086-5. *Leader Guide,* item 0-7673-9085-7.
- *In God's Presence, Youth Edition* by T. W. Hunt is a six-week, interactive course designed for daily personal study and weekly group meetings. Item 0-7673-0001-7.

### Adult

- *Disciple's Prayer Life: Walking in Fellowship with God* by T. W. Hunt and Catherine Walker is a comprehensive, interactive, 13-week study designed for daily personal study and weekly group meetings. *Member Book,* item 0-7673-3494-9. A video package consists of four videotapes featuring T. W. Hunt teaching his material in 13 sessions, item 0-8054-8397-7.
- *The Life-Changing Power of Prayer* by T. W. Hunt is an in-depth study of prayer. The six-chapter book is designed for members to read at home, then discuss in a group at church. Item 0-6330-1980-1.
- *Experiencing God* by Henry T. Blackaby and Claude V. King is a scriptural study of how to know and do God's will. *Member Book,* item 0-8054-9954-7. *Leader Guide,* item 0-8054-9951-2. Hardcover book edition, item 7810-0-8054-0196-2. Softcover book edition, item 7811-0-8054-0197-0.

- *In God's Presence* by T. W. Hunt and Claude V. King is a six-week, interactive study designed for daily personal study and weekly group meetings. Item 0-8054-9900-8.
- *Watchman Prayer Ministry* by Larry L. Thompson presents a plan that mobilizes a church to pray continuously for its needs and for revival. *Planning Kit,* item 0-8054-9960-1. *Prayer Guide,* item 0-8054-9962-8.
- *The Prayer of Jesus: Living the Lord's Prayer* by Ken Hemphill helps believers live the truths Jesus taught in the Lord's Prayer. *Member Book,* item 0-6330-7624-4. *Leader Kit,* item 0-6330-7623-6

### Language Editions
- *In God's Presence, Spanish Edition* by T. W. Hunt is a six-week, interactive course designed for daily personal study and weekly group meetings. Item 0-8054-9699-8.

## Ordering Information

To order prayer resources, write to Customer Service Center; One LifeWay Plaza; Nashville, TN 37234-0113; call (800) 458-2772; fax (615) 251-5933; e-mail *customerservice@lifeway.com;* order online at *www.lifeway.com;* or visit a LifeWay Christian Store.

## Web Site

*www.lifeway.com* provides information about resources and upcoming conferences on prayer, as well as on other areas of discipleship.

## Prayer Specialist

LifeWay Christian Resources provides a national prayer consultant to help churches become houses of prayer. Call John Franklin, (615) 251-5620, or e-mail *john.franklin@lifeway.com.*

---

**NORTH AMERICAN MISSION BOARD**

The North American Mission Board has two assignments that particularly relate to prayer: spiritual awakening and evangelism.

## Vision Statements for Prayer

### Spiritual Awakening
Our mission is to help churches and associations pray for revival, to help them better understand the nature of true revival, to provide information on recognizing and responding to inadequate or false revival, and to provide scriptural guidelines for preparation for true revival.

### Evangelism
Our mission is to lead churches and associations to pray for and share Jesus with every person in their spheres of influence.

These visions are accomplished by cooperating with churches, associations, state conventions, and Southern Baptist entities to develop contextual approaches for prayer and renewal strategies, methods, and materials.

## Objectives

1. To reclaim or renew a personal passion to pray unceasingly (see 1 Thess. 5:17)
2. To reclaim or renew the church as a house of prayer with a passion for the lost (see Matt. 21:13; Luke 19:10)
3. To link believers in focused, united prayer for evangelization and awakening (see 2 Chron. 7:14; 1 Tim. 2:1-4)

## Resources

### Prayer and Spiritual Awakening

- *The Heart of the Problem* presents Christ as the only answer for human sin. Only true repentance can bring healing in our lives. Item 0-8054-1667-6.
- *The Power of the Call* is designed to draw pastors and leaders back to their original calls to ministry. Item 0-8054-6297-X.
- Recommended reading list suggests resources for reading and study on various subjects pertaining to prayer, holiness, and revival.
- Regional conferences/seminars are conducted across the nation that focus on preparation for revival.
- *Return to Worship* reveals the Who of worship, why we worship, and how to worship a holy and awesome God. Item 0-8054-1888-1.
- *Fresh Encounter: God's Pattern for Revival and Spiritual Awakening* by Henry T. Blackaby and Claude V. King outlines the biblical pattern for revival by directing Christians to the Scriptures and to God in prayer. *God's Pattern for Revival and Spiritual Awakening, Member Book 1,* item 0-8054-9920-2. *Leader Manual,* item 0-8054-9921-0. *Leader Kit,* item 0-8054-9898-2. *A Plumb Line for God's People, Member Book 2,* item 0-8054-9919-9.
- *www.oneinamillion.com.* To encourage one accord praying for revival and spiritual awakening through a weekly prayer focus, daily prayer guide, inspiring articles, and current stories of what God is doing.

### Prayer and Evangelism

- *Great Commission Prayer Strategy* booklet is an informative source for principles and procedures to create a Great Commission prayer strategy in a church.
- Lighthouse of Prayer lapel pin is an attractive conversation starter for those who commit to make their homes lighthouses of prayer. Item 0-8400-9625-9, pack of 10.
- *Lighthouse of Prayer Starter Kit* equips families to pray, care, and share with their neighbors. Item 0-8400-9682-8.

- *On Mission as a Lighthouse of Prayer* informational/recruitment brochure explains the need and rewards for making each home a lighthouse of prayer in a churchwide prayer strategy. Item 0-8400-8567-2, pack of 50.
- On-Mission Prayer Map is a beautiful guide to daily prayer for believers and unbelievers by state or province.
- *Prayer Guide for Associations and Churches* is a helpful guide to associational prayer coordinators who are seeking to lead their churches in Great Commission praying.
- *Praying Your Friend to Christ* tract is a companion prayer-triad piece that provides a brief explanation of praying for the lost. Item 0-8400-6728-3, pack of 100.
- *Praying Your Friend to Christ Training Guide* is a practical tool for learning how to focus prayer on the lost. Item 0-8400-8837-X.
- *Taking Prayer to the Streets: Prayer Journeys Guidebook* is a compact booklet that helps guide prayer for field teams and support teams. Item 0-8400-9637-2, pack of 25.
- *Taking Prayer to the Streets: Prayer Journeys Resource Kit* instructs and trains lighthouse-of-prayer participants to hold prayer journeys. Item 0-8400-9632-1.

## Ordering Information

Items listed with item numbers are available from Customer Service Center; One LifeWay Plaza; Nashville, TN 37234-0113; call (800) 448-8032; fax (615) 251-5983; e-mail *customerservice@lifeway.com;* order online at *www.lifeway.com.* Direct other inquiries to Prayer Evangelism Unit; the North American Mission Board; 4200 North Point Parkway; Alpharetta, GA 30022-4176; (770) 410-6333.

## Web Site

*www.namb.net/prayer* is an online resource that provides information and links to help create a Great Commission prayer strategy and implementation plan.

## WOMAN'S MISSIONARY UNION

## Vision Statement for Prayer

Woman's Missionary Union (WMU) challenges Christian believers to understand and be radically involved in the mission of God through prayer.

WMU has been committed to involving persons in missions and supporting the Southern Baptist missions effort since 1888. Prayer is central to that commitment, the success of missions, and the vitality of the Christian life. A priority in the missions-education organizations and ministries of WMU is prayer—prayer for missions and missionaries, as well as a Christian believer's development of a healthy prayer life.

## Resources

Many resources are available to encourage churches, WMU members, and others to be active in prayer and to grow in their prayer lives.

### Books
- *Follow Me—Lessons for Becoming a Prayer-walker* by Randy Sprinkle is a tool that will transform a willing believer into an effective prayerwalker. Item 1-5630-9718-4.
- *Legacy of Prayer—A Spiritual Trust Fund for the Generations* by Jennifer Kennedy Dean. Prayer is not merely a tradition to pass down, but a time-transcendent power that dramatically transforms the hearts and lives of generations to come. Item 1-5630-9711-7.
- *The Life That Prays* by Minette Drumwright guides readers to experience prayer that has an impact on all aspects of life. Item 1-5630-9489-4.
- *Live a Praying Life* by Jennifer Kennedy Dean answers questions that concern prayer and offers a glimpse into God's plan to include us in accomplishing His will. Item 1-56309-091-0.
- *Riches Stored in Secret Places* by Jennifer Kennedy Dean is a 12-week devotional guide designed to deepen a spiritual relationship with the Father. Item 1-5630-9752-4.

### Magazines
Monthly or quarterly WMU magazines regularly promote and provide instruction about prayer with various age and language groups. These resources give strong attention to praying for missions and missionaries.
- *Acteens Leadership* (for Acteens—teenage girls)
- *Aware* (Girls in Action leadership)
- *Mission Leader* (church leadership/associational leadership)
- *Discovery* (for Girls in Action—younger girls)
- *GA World* (for Girls in Action—older girls)
- *Missions Matchfile for Children in Action* (for Children in Action directors to use with girls and boys in grades 1–6)
- *Missions Mosaic* (for women)
- *Nuestra Tarea* (Spanish for Hispanic churches)
- *The Mag* (teenage girls)
- *Share* (Missions Friends leaflet for parents)
- *Start* (Missions Friends leadership)
- *Youth on Mission* (for Youth on Mission—teenage girls and boys; an annual resource for Youth on Mission leaders or youth leaders)

## Ordering Information

Print resources can be obtained through the online bookstore at *www.wmu.com*. Books and monthly or quarterly magazines can be obtained by calling WMU Customer Service, (800) 968-7301. Books can also be purchased at LifeWay Christian Stores.

## Web Site

*www.wmu.com* highlights important areas of prayer.

## WMU Consultants

On national and state levels, WMU leaders are available to assist churches in involving persons in prayer through prayer retreats and experiences. Contact Woman's Missionary Union; 100 Missionary Ridge; Birmingham, AL 35283-0100; (205) 991-8100.

CHAPTER

# 7

CHAPTER

# PRAYER RESOURCES *And* NETWORKS

## JOHN FRANKLIN

### PARACHURCH PRAYER ORGANIZATIONS

### Bible-Based Praying

**Contact**
Don Miller; P.O. Box 8911; Fort Worth, TX 76124; call (817) 429-6917.

**Purpose**
To train all Christians in praying, especially targeting the local church

**Method**
Conferences are led in the local church, complete with overhead-cel presentation and viewing guide for conference participants.

### The Capitol Hill Prayer Alert

**Contact**
P.O. Box 7334; Arlington, VA 22207; call (540) 878-2125; fax (540) 878-2126; visit *www.prayeralert.org.*

**Purpose**
To alert Christians to political concerns that affect the nation

**Method**
Updates are distributed through fax and/or e-mail for intercessors' personal use or for churches.

### Concerts of Prayer International

**Contact**
P.O. Box 770; New Providence, NJ 07974; call (877) NOW-HOPE; visit *www.nationalprayer.org.*

**Purpose**
To mobilize prayer for spiritual awakening and world evangelization

**Method**
Citywide prayer rallies are sponsored in cooperation with pastors. Resources are provided to facilitate organized prayer.

### Evelyn Christenson Ministries, Inc., and United Prayer Ministry

**Contact**
P.O. Box 120886; Saint Paul, MN 55112; call (763) 566-5390; *www.unitedprayerministry.org.*

**Purpose**
To teach women to pray

**Method**
Books, resources, conferences

## Every Home for Christ

**Contact**
P.O. Box 64000; Colorado Springs, CO 80962; call (800) 423-5054; e-mail *info@ehc.org;* visit *www.ehc.org.*

**Purpose**
To mobilize Christians to pray for and actively participate in personally presenting the gospel to every home in the world

**Method**
Network with other ministries to train and organize door-to-door campaigns through training conferences and resources.

## Harvest Prayer Ministries

**Contact**
619 Washington Ave.; Terre Haute, IN 47802 call (812) 238-5504; visit *www.harvestprayer.com.*

**Purpose**
To mobilize the church in the ministry of prayer.

**Method**
Teaching others why and how to pray for a spiritual awakening of the church.

## Houses of Prayer Everywhere

**Contact**
455 W. Springhill Road; Terre Haute, IN 47802; call (800) 217-5200; fax (812) 235-6646; e-mail *info@hopeministries.org;* visit *www.hopeministries.org.*
**Purpose**
To mobilize community prayer cells of from four to six persons to pray for neighbors

**Method**
Provide training through conferences and/or resources.

## Intercessors for America

**Contact**
192 N. 21st St.; Purcellville, VA 20132-3077; call (540) 751-0980; visit *www.ifa-usapray.org.*

**Purpose**
To mobilize prayer for national leaders and for spiritual awakening

**Method**
Mail monthly newsletter and weekly prayer alert via fax and e-mail.

## International Awakening Ministries

**Contact**
P.O. Box 232; Wheaton, IL 60189-0232; call (630) 653-8616; visit *www.intl-awaken.com*

**Purpose**
To promote prayer for spiritual awakening

**Method**
Books, seminars, speaking engagements

## International Prayer Ministries, Inc.

**Contact**
3322 Irwin Bridge Road, NW; Conyers, GA 30012-2033; call (770) 483-6603; fax (770) 483-8606; e-mail *gshep10143@cs.com.*

**Purpose**
To mobilize prayer for personal revival, spiritual awakening, and world evangelization

**Method**
Conferences, prayer revivals, books, and tapes

## Life Action Ministries

**Contact**
P.O. Box 31; Buchanan, MI 49107-0031; call (269) 684-5905; fax (269) 695-2474; e-mail *info@lifeaction.org;* visit *www.lifeaction.org.*

**Purpose**
To lead churches in spiritual renewal

**Method**
Trained teams present a multimedia combination of drama, video, and speaking on topics necessary to spiritual renewal.

## Lydia Fellowship International

**Contact**
P.O. Box 15118; Washington, DC 20003; *www.lydiafellowship.org.*

**Purpose**
To mobilize women to intercede primarily for cities, states, America, and the nations of the world

**Method**
Create a national network of intercessors, provide conferences, and print prayer resources.

## March for Jesus

**Contact**
P.O. Box 35976; Richmond, VA 23235; call (804) 745-8400; fax (215) 895-9984; e-mail *info@jesusday.org;* visit *www.jesusday.org.*

**Purpose**
To mobilize a nationwide prayerwalk in the spring with an emphasis on praise

**Method**
Resources, training conferences, and Web site

## Mission America Coalition

**Contact**
P.O. Box 13930; Palm Desert, CA 92255; call (760) 200-2707; fax (760) 200-8837; e-mail *info@mission-america.org;* visit *missionamerica.org* and *lighthousemovement.com.*

**Purpose**
To mobilize all denominations in a national, unified effort to pray for, care for, and share Christ with every person in America

**Method**
Encourage believers to be lighthouses to neighbors and coworkers through a prayer, care, and share strategy.

## Moms in Touch International

**Contact**
P.O. Box 1120; Poway, CA 92074-1120; call (800) 949-MOMS; visit *momsintouch.org.*

**Purpose**
To mobilize moms to pray together for their children's schools

**Method**
Printed resources

## National Day of Prayer Task Force

**Contact**
P.O. Box 15616; Colorado Springs, CO 80935-5616; call (719) 531-3379; fax (719) 548-4520; order (800) 444-8828; visit *www.nationaldayofprayer.org.*

**Purpose**
To lead and coordinate efforts for the National Day of Prayer

**Method**
Provide resources churches can use to mobilize their members to prayer.

## Nationally Broadcast Concert of Prayer

**Contact**
901 East 78th Street; Minneapolis, MN 55420-1334; call (952) 853-8448; visit *www.concertofprayer.org.*

**Purpose**
To provide impetus for the National Day of Prayer

**Method**
This event is a three-hour live television, radio, Internet, and satellite simulcast concert of prayer held on the evening of the National Day of Prayer.

## National Pastors' Prayer Network

**Contact**
1130 E. Randville Dr.; Palatine, IL 60074-2925; call (847) 991-0227; e-mail *phil@nppn.org;* visit *www.nppn.org.*

**Purpose**
To network pastors to pray together in encouragement and prayer support

**Method**

Utilize e-mail to connect pastors and keep them abreast of what is happening among pastors around the nation.

## *Pray!* Magazine

**Contact**

NavPress; P.O. Box 35002; Colorado Springs, CO 80935; call (719) 531-3555; visit *www.praymag.com.*

**Purpose**

To provide a magazine focusing solely on prayer

**Method**

Mail subscribers six issues a year.

## PrayerPower Ministries

**Contact**

P.O. Box 801368; Dallas, TX 75380; call (800) 949-PRAY; visit *www.learntopray.org.*

**Purpose**

To train Christians in prayer

**Method**

Conferences and printed resources

## RENOVARÉ

**Contact**

8 Inverness Drive, East, Suite 102; Englewood, CO 80112-5624; call (303) 792-0152; fax (303) 792-0146; e-mail *contact@renovare.org;* visit *www.renovare.org.*

**Purpose**

To help churches in spiritual renewal through the practice of six spiritual disciplines

**Method**

Conferences, books, small-group resources

## Sammy Tippit Ministries

**Contact**

P.O. Box 781767; San Antonio, TX 78278; call 1-210-492-7501; fax: 1-210-492-4522; visit *www.sammytippit.org.*

**Purpose**

Exists to glorify God by evangelizing the world for Christ.

**Method**

Equip and impart vision and a passion for the lost to church leaders in such a way that it results in outreach and impacts both cities and nations for Christ with long-term results.

## See You at the Pole

**Contact**

P.O. Box 60134; Fort Worth, TX 76115; call (817) 447-7526; visit *www.syatp.com.*

**Purpose**

To mobilize youth across the nation to participate in unified prayer one day a year

**Method**

Use resources, videos, and Web site to encourage youth to pray at their schools' flagpoles on the third Wednesday in September.

## Waymakers

**Contact**

Waymakers, Box 203131; Austin, Texas 78720-3131; (800) 264-5214; visit *www.waymakers.org.*

**Purpose:**

WayMakers is a mobilization ministry focused on seeing Christ glorified by obedient, worshiping movements in every people group.

**Method**

Saturating a city or a relational setting with prayer through a one-time event or project

---

**PRAYER RESOURCES**

## Aids to Church Prayer Life

Blackaby, Henry T., and Claude V. King. *Experiencing God.* Nashville: LifeWay, 1990.

———. *Fresh Encounter.* Nashville: LifeWay, 1993.

Hawthorne, Steve. *Prayerwalking: Praying on Site with Insight.* Lake Mary, FL: Creation House, 1993.

Hunt, T. W., and Claude V. King. *In God's Presence.* Nashville: LifeWay, 1994.

Hunt, T. W., and Claude V. King. *The Mind of Christ*. Nashville: LifeWay, 1994.

Johnstone, Patrick. *Operation World*. Grand Rapids: Zondervan, 1993.

Thompson, Larry L. *Watchman Intercessory Prayer Ministry*. Nashville: LifeWay, 1992.

Vander Griend, Alvin. *Church Lighthouse Kit*. Grand Rapids: HOPE Ministries, 1999.

Vander Griend, Alvin, and Edith Bayena. *Praying Church Sourcebook*. Grand Rapids: CRC, 1997.

Willis, Avery T., Jr. *MasterLife*. Nashville: LifeWay, 1996–97.

## Biographies

Carre, E. G. *Praying Hyde: The Life of John "Praying" Hyde*. North Brunswick, NJ: Bridge-Logos, 1983.

Grubb, Norman. *C. T. Studd*. Fort Washington, PA: Christian Literature Crusade, 1991.

———. *Rees Howells: Intercessor*. Fort Washington, PA: Christian Literature Crusade, 1952.

Howard, Philip E. *The Life and Diary of David Brainerd*. Grand Rapids: Baker, 1989.

Mueller, George. *The Autobiography of George Mueller*. New Kensington, PA: Whitaker, 1984.

Taylor, Howard, and Mary G. Taylor. *Hudson Taylor's Spiritual Secret*. Chicago: Moody, 1987.

## Books

Blackaby, Henry T., and Claude V. King. *Experiencing God*. Nashville: Broadman & Holman, 1994.

Bounds, E. M. *Power Through Prayer*. New Kensington, PA: Whitaker, 1983.

———. *The Reality of Prayer*. Ada, MI: Baker, 1992.

Chambers, Oswald. *If You Will Ask*. Fort Washington, PA: Christian Literature Crusade, 1985.

Christenson, Evelyn. *What Happens When Women Pray?* Colorado Springs: Chariot Victor, 1992.

Cymbala, Jim. *Fresh Wind, Fresh Fire*. Grand Rapids: Zondervan, 1997.

Deweese, Charles. *Prayer in Baptist Life*. Nashville: Broadman, 1986.

Duewel, Wesley. *Mighty Prevailing Prayer*. Grand Rapids: Zondervan, 1990.

———. *Touch the World Through Prayer*. Grand Rapids: Zondervan, 1986.

Forsythe, P. T. *The Soul of Prayer*. Salem, OH: Schmul, 1986.

Gordon, S. D. *Quiet Talks on Prayer*. Minneapolis: Bethany Fellowship, 1986.

Guyon, Madame. *Experiencing God Through Prayer*. New Kensington, PA: Whitaker, 1984.

Hallesby, Ole. *Prayer*. Minneapolis: Augsburg, 1959.

Huegel, F. J. *The Ministry of Intercession*. Minneapolis: Bethany Fellowship, 1976.

———. *Prayer's Deeper Secrets: Successful Praying*. Minneapolis: Bethany Fellowship, 1967.

Hunt, T. W. *The Life-Changing Power of Prayer*. Nashville: Convention, 2002.

———. *The Mind of Christ*. Nashville: Broadman & Holman, 1995.

Lawrence, Brother. *The Practice of the Presence of God*. Ashland City, TN: Brightside, 1996.

Lord, Peter. *Hearing God*. Ada, MI: Baker, 1988.

Moody, D. L. *Prevailing Prayer*. Chicago: Moody, 1984.

Mueller, George. *Answers to Prayer*. Chicago: Moody, 1984.

Murray, Andrew. *The Ministry of Intercession: A Plea for More Prayer*. Grand Rapids: Zondervan, 1987.

———. *With Christ in the School of Prayer*. New Kensington, PA: Whitaker House, 1981.

Stanley, Charles. *Handle with Prayer*. Colorado Springs: Chariot Victor, 1992.

Tozer, A. W. *The Pursuit of God*. Camp Hill, PA: Christian Publications, 1995.

Wallis, Arthur. *God's Chosen Fast*. Fort Washington, PA: Christian Literature Crusade, 1986.

## Devotionals

Chambers, Oswald. *My Utmost for His Highest*. Uhrichsville, OH: Barbour, 1999.

*Journey: A Woman's Guide to Intimacy with God* magazine. Write to Customer Service Center; One LifeWay Plaza; Nashville, TN 37234-0113; fax (615) 251-5933; call toll free (800) 458-2772; e-mail *customerservice@lifeway.com;* order online at *www.lifeway.com.*

Moore, Beth. *Whispers of Hope*. Nashville: LifeWay, 1998.

*Stand Firm: God's Challenge for Today's Man* magazine. Write to Customer Service Center;

One LifeWay Plaza; Nashville, TN 37234-0113; fax (615) 251-5933; call toll free (800) 458-2772; e-mail *customerservice@lifeway.com;* order online at *www.lifeway.com.*

Willis, Avery. T., Jr., and J. David Carter. *Day by Day in God's Kingdom: A Discipleship Journal.* Nashville: LifeWay, 1997.

## Group Discipleship Studies

Blackaby, Henry T., and Claude V. King. *Experiencing God.* Nashville: LifeWay, 1990.

———. *Fresh Encounter.* Nashville: LifeWay, 1993.

Hunt, T. W., and Catherine Walker. *Disciple's Prayer Life.* Nashville: LifeWay, 1997.

Hunt, T. W., and Claude V. King. *In God's Presence.* Nashville: LifeWay, 1994.

———. *The Mind of Christ.* Nashville: LifeWay, 1994.

McQuilkin, Robertson. *Life in the Spirit.* Nashville: LifeWay, 1997.

Willis, Avery T., Jr. *MasterLife.* Nashville: LifeWay, 1996–97.

## Magazine

*Pray!* magazine. NavPress; P.O. Box 35002; Colorado Springs, CO 80935; call (719) 531-3555; visit *www.praymag.com.*

## Programs

Maxwell, John. *Partners in Prayer.* Nashville: Thomas Nelson, 1996.

Thompson, Larry L. *Watchman Intercessory Prayer Ministry.* Nashville: LifeWay, 1992.

Vander Griend, Alvin. *Church Lighthouse Kit.* Grand Rapids: HOPE Ministries, 1999.

## Spiritual Awakening

Blackaby, Henry T., and Claude V. King. *Fresh Encounter.* Nashville: Broadman & Holman, 1996.

Culpepper, C. L. *The Shantung Revival.* Alpharetta, GA: The North American Mission Board of the Southern Baptist Convention, 1982.

Duewel, Wesley. *Revival Fire!* Grand Rapids: Zondervan, 1995.

Edwards, Brian. *Revival: A People Saturated with God.* Darlington County, Durham: Evangelical, 1990.

Edwards, Jonathan. *On Revival.* Carlisle, PA: Banner of Truth, 1984.

Eklund, Bob. *Spiritual Awakening.* Alpharetta, GA: The North American Mission Board of the Southern Baptist Convention, 1986.

Greenfield, John. *The Power from on High: The Story of the Great Moravian Revival of 1727.* Bethlehem, PA: Moravian Church in America, 1997.

Hession, Roy. *Calvary Road.* Fort Washington, PA: Christian Literature Crusade, 1997.

Hunter, John. *Knowing God's Secrets.* Kingsport, TN: Fresh Springs, 1995.

Lloyd-Jones, D. Martin. *Revival.* Wheaton, IL: Crossway, 1987.

Lewis, Jessie Penn. *The Awakening in Wales.* Fort Washington, PA: Christian Literature Crusade, 1993.

Olford, Stephen. *Heart Cry for Revival.* Memphis: Encounter Ministries, 1987.

———. *Not I but Christ.* Wheaton, IL: Crossway, 1997.

Orr, Edwin, J. *Campus Aflame: A History of Evangelical Awakenings in Collegiate Communities.* Wheaton, IL: International Awakening, 1994.

Owens, Ron. *Return to Worship: Letters to the Church.* Nashville: LifeWay, 1999.

Fehsenfeld, Del, Jr. *Ablaze with His Glory.* Nashville: Thomas Nelson, 1993.

Ravenhill, Leonard. *Revival Praying.* Minneapolis: Bethany House, 1962.

———. *Why Revival Tarries.* Minneapolis: Bethany House, 1979.

———. *America Is Too Young to Die.* Minneapolis: Bethany House, 1979.

Roberts, Richard Owen. *Revival.* Wheaton, IL: Richard Owen Roberts, 1991.

Stewart, James. *Opened Windows.* Asheville, NC: Revival Literature, 1958.

Note: Resources that are no longer in print may be found at your church library, associational office, or state convention office.

## Prayer Request

_____ Church's intercessory prayer room provides one of our most vital support ministries. The intercessory prayer room is staffed _____ hours a day by volunteer prayer warriors. The intercessory prayer-room ministry serves as a prayer-support system for our church family; our staff; and people throughout our city, state, nation, and world.

If you would like to learn how you can become a part of this exciting ministry, please contact the intercessory prayer-room office at _____ or complete the information below. Then place this card in the offering plate, drop it in a prayer-request box, or bring it by the intercessory prayer room.

Name: _____
Address: _____
City: _____ State: _____
ZIP: _____
Home phone: _____
Work phone: _____

## GOD _Answers_ PRAYER

**INTERCESSORY PRAYER ROOM**
[Your church's name, address, and prayer line]

---

_Be anxious for nothing, but in everything by prayer and supplication, with thanksgiving, let your requests be made known to God; and the peace of God, which surpasses all understanding, will guard your hearts and minds through Christ Jesus_ (Phil. 4:6-7).

**Person needing prayer:**

Name: _____     Date: _____
Address: _____     **Check one:**
City: _____ State: _____ ZIP: _____     ❏ New request
Is this person a member of our church? ❏ Yes ❏ No ❏ Not sure     ❏ Answer to previous request
Is this person a Christian? ❏ Yes ❏ No ❏ Not sure     ❏ Update to previous request
May we send this person a note of encouragement? ❏ Yes ❏ No

Prayer request: _____
_____
_____

**Person making request:**

Name: _____
Address: _____
City: _____ State: _____ ZIP: _____
Home phone: _____ Work phone: _____

Relationship to person being prayed for: _____

**PLACE THIS CARD IN THE OFFERING PLATE, DROP IT IN A PRAYER-REQUEST BOX, OR BRING IT BY THE INTERCESSORY PRAYER ROOM**

Prayer-Request Card

Person being prayed for: _____

Brief review of situation: _____

_____

_____

FIRST LETTER

☐

OF LAST NAME

Category:

_____

_____

**Prayer-room use only**

Prayer request: _____

_____

_____

_____

_____

_____

_____

Please complete the information on back. Update information at least every 30 days to keep your request active.

Person making request: _____

Phone: _____  Date: _____

Would this person like a note of encouragement? ☐ Yes ☐ No ☐ Not sure
If so, give the person's address:

Name: _____

Address: _____

City: _____

State: _____  ZIP: _____

Dates prayergrams or emails sent:

|   |   |   |   |
|---|---|---|---|
|   |   |   |   |
|   |   |   |   |
|   |   |   |   |

**Prayer-room use only**

May an intercessor verbally and privately encourage this person?
☐ Yes ☐ No
Is the person being prayed for a member of our church?
☐ Yes ☐ No ☐ Not sure
Is this request also for salvation?
☐ Yes ☐ No ☐ Not sure

## ALL PRAYER REQUESTS ARE CONSIDERED CONFIDENTIAL

**Date**

_____ / _____ / _____
Month    Day    Year

**Time**

_____ a.m.

_____ p.m.

Send a prayergram?
❏ Yes   ❏ No
    Date       Initials

**Pray for:**
Name: _____

Address: _____

City: _____ State: _____ ZIP: _____

**Christian**
❏ Yes   ❏ No   ❏ Not sure
**Member**
❏ Yes   ❏ No   ❏ Not sure
Relationship to member

_____

### Prayer Request and/or Update
Use red ink for answered prayers, green for updates. Use back of card if needed.

_____
_____
_____
_____
_____
_____
_____
_____
_____

**Prayer requested by:** Name: _____

Address: _____ City: _____

State: _____ ZIP: _____ Phone: _____

Member: ❏ Yes   ❏ No

Recorded by

_____

---

**Date**

_____ / _____ / _____
Month    Day    Year

**Time**

_____ a.m.

_____ p.m.

Send a prayergram?
❏ Yes   ❏ No
    Date       Initials

**Pray for:**
Name: _____

Address: _____

City: _____ State: _____ ZIP: _____

**Christian**
❏ Yes   ❏ No   ❏ Not sure
**Member**
❏ Yes   ❏ No   ❏ Not sure
Relationship to member

_____

### Prayer Request and/or Update
Use red ink for answered prayers, green for updates. Use back of card if needed.

_____
_____
_____
_____
_____
_____
_____
_____
_____

**Prayer requested by:** Name: _____

Address: _____ City: _____

State: _____ ZIP: _____ Phone: _____

Member: ❏ Yes   ❏ No

Recorded by

_____

Telephone-Request Ca

*Praying ... for me, that utterance may be given to me, that I may open my mouth boldly to make known the mystery of the gospel (Eph. 6:18-19).*

Staff member's name: _____ Date: _____

Scripture claimed: _____

_____

Personal requests: _____

_____

_____

_____

Family requests: _____

_____

_____

_____

Ministry requests: _____

_____

_____

_____

_____

Praise: _____

_____

_____

Dear _____,

You and your request for _____
have been in our prayers here in the intercessory prayer room. We
will continue to pray for you. Please let us know of any change in
your request or ways God has answered our prayers. Because your
request is important to us, we want our prayers to be based on
up-to-date information.

Thank you for your request. You may call [your church's prayer
line] anytime with a request or an update.

In Christ,

_____

Intercessory Prayer Room

[Your church's name
  and address]

[Your church's name
and address]

I... do not cease to
give thanks for you,
making mention of you
in my prayers.

Ephesians 1:15-16

PRAYERGRAM

INTERCESSORY PRAYER ROOM

PRAYER LINE: _____

*Be still, and know
that I am God.*
Psalm 46:10

REJOICING IN HOPE, PATIENT IN TRIBULATION,
CONTINUING STEADFASTLY IN PRAYER (ROM. 12:12).

Prayergram

# PRAYERGRAM

*Whatever things you ask in prayer, believing, you will receive.*
Matthew 21:22

*Pray without ceasing.*
1 Thessalonians 5:17

*Pray for one another.*
James 5:16

**Intercessory Prayer Room**

[Your church's name and address]

**24-Hour Prayer Line**

[Your prayer line's number]

**A Ministry of**

[Your church's name]

*My house is a house of prayer.*
Luke 19:46

GOD ANSWERS PRAYER

[Your church's name and address]

# DAILY SIGN-IN SHEET

Date: _____

| Time | |
|---|---|
| 12:00–1:00 a.m. | _____ |
| 1:00–2:00 a.m. | _____ |
| 2:00–3:00 a.m. | _____ |
| 3:00–4:00 a.m. | _____ |
| 4:00–5:00 a.m. | _____ |
| 5:00–6:00 a.m. | _____ |
| 6:00–7:00 a.m. | _____ |
| 7:00–8:00 a.m. | _____ |
| 8:00–9:00 a.m. | _____ |
| 9:00–10:00 a.m. | _____ |
| 10:00–11:00 a.m. | _____ |
| 11:00 a.m.–12:00 p.m. | _____ |
| 12:00–1:00 p.m. | _____ |
| 1:00–2:00 p.m. | _____ |
| 2:00–3:00 p.m. | _____ |
| 3:00–4:00 p.m. | _____ |
| 4:00–5:00 p.m. | _____ |
| 5:00–6:00 p.m. | _____ |
| 6:00–7:00 p.m. | _____ |
| 7:00–8:00 p.m. | _____ |
| 8:00–9:00 p.m. | _____ |
| 9:00–10:00 p.m. | _____ |
| 10:00–11:00 p.m. | _____ |
| 11:00 p.m.–12:00 a.m. | _____ |

*Continue earnestly in prayer, being vigilant in it with thanksgiving.*
Colossians 4:2

Care leader _____

| | Sunday | Monday | Tuesday | Wednesday | Thursday | Friday | Saturday |
|---|---|---|---|---|---|---|---|
| 12:00–1:00 a.m. | | | | | | | |
| 1:00–2:00 a.m. | | | | | | | |
| 2:00–3:00 a.m. | | | | | | | |
| 3:00–4:00 a.m. | | | | | | | |
| 4:00–5:00 a.m. | | | | | | | |
| 5:00–6:00 a.m. | | | | | | | |
| 6:00–7:00 a.m. | | | | | | | |
| 7:00–8:00 a.m. | | | | | | | |
| 8:00–9:00 a.m. | | | | | | | |
| 9:00–10:00 a.m. | | | | | | | |
| 10:00–11:00 a.m. | | | | | | | |
| 11:00 a.m.–12:00 p.m. | | | | | | | |

Care leader _____

| | Sunday | Monday | Tuesday | Wednesday | Thursday | Friday | Saturday |
|---|---|---|---|---|---|---|---|
| 12:00–1:00 p.m. | | | | | | | |
| 1:00–2:00 p.m. | | | | | | | |
| 2:00–3:00 p.m. | | | | | | | |
| 3:00–4:00 p.m. | | | | | | | |
| 4:00–5:00 p.m. | | | | | | | |
| 5:00–6:00 p.m. | | | | | | | |
| 6:00–7:00 p.m. | | | | | | | |
| 7:00–8:00 p.m. | | | | | | | |
| 8:00–9:00 p.m. | | | | | | | |
| 9:00–10:00 p.m. | | | | | | | |
| 10:00–11:00 p.m. | | | | | | | |
| 11:00 p.m.–12:00 a.m. | | | | | | | |

## INTERCESSORY PRAYER-ROOM COMMITMENT

Name: _____ Birth month and day: _____

Address: _____

City: _____ State: _____ ZIP: _____

Home phone: _____ Work phone: _____

First choice, day and hour: _____ Second choice: _____

Are you a member of a class or group? ❑ Yes ❑ No  Which one? _____

Contact person for your class or group: _____

*By making this commitment, I agree to cover my assigned hour regularly. I understand that we as intercessors are not counselors and should refer persons needing help to a trained counselor. I will refrain from making promises that the church cannot keep. I also understand that all prayer requests are confidential.*

**Signed** _____

---

## INTERCESSORY PRAYER-ROOM COMMITMENT

Name: _____ Birth month and day: _____

Address: _____

City: _____ State: _____ ZIP: _____

Home phone: _____ Work phone: _____

First choice, day and hour: _____ Second choice: _____

Are you a member of a class or group? ❑ Yes ❑ No  Which one? _____

Contact person for your class or group: _____

*By making this commitment, I agree to cover my assigned hour regularly. I understand that we as intercessors are not counselors and should refer persons needing help to a trained counselor. I will refrain from making promises that the church cannot keep. I also understand that all prayer requests are confidential.*

**Signed** _____

## ENROLLMENT SHEET

| | Sunday | Monday | Tuesday | Wednesday | Thursday | Friday | Saturday |
|---|---|---|---|---|---|---|---|
| 12:00–1:00 a.m. | | | | | | | |
| 1:00–2:00 a.m. | | | | | | | |
| 2:00–3:00 a.m. | | | | | | | |
| 3:00–4:00 a.m. | | | | | | | |
| 4:00–5:00 a.m. | | | | | | | |
| 5:00–6:00 a.m. | | | | | | | |
| 6:00–7:00 a.m. | | | | | | | |
| 7:00–8:00 a.m. | | | | | | | |
| 8:00–9:00 a.m. | | | | | | | |
| 9:00–10:00 a.m. | | | | | | | |
| 10:00–11:00 a.m. | | | | | | | |
| 11:00 a.m.–12:00 p.m. | | | | | | | |
| 12:00–1:00 p.m. | | | | | | | |
| 1:00–2:00 p.m. | | | | | | | |
| 2:00–3:00 p.m. | | | | | | | |
| 3:00–4:00 p.m. | | | | | | | |
| 4:00–5:00 p.m. | | | | | | | |
| 5:00–6:00 p.m. | | | | | | | |
| 6:00–7:00 p.m. | | | | | | | |
| 7:00–8:00 p.m. | | | | | | | |
| 8:00–9:00 p.m. | | | | | | | |
| 9:00–10:00 p.m. | | | | | | | |
| 10:00–11:00 p.m. | | | | | | | |
| 11:00 p.m.–12:00 a.m. | | | | | | | |

THIS INFORMATION CAN BE ENLARGED ON A DRY-ERASE OR MAGNETIC BOARD

Week of _____    Number of hours filled: _____

Number of prayergrams mailed: _____

Number of telephone calls received:

    Calls from church members: _____

        Calls from nonmembers: _____

New intercessors this week: _____

_____

_____

New or additional training provided for: _____

_____

_____

Intercessors I wrote or called to encourage: _____

_____

_____

Projects I worked on this week: _____

_____

_____

Names of members, prospects, or family members with requests the pastor should know about:

_____

_____

_____

_____

# CARE LEADER'S MONTHLY REPORT

Month: _____

Day: _____

Care leader: _____

| Hour | Name | Week 1 | Week 2 | Week 3 | Week 4 | Week 5 | Comments |
|------|------|--------|--------|--------|--------|--------|----------|
| 12:00–1:00 | | | | | | | |
| 1:00–2:00 | | | | | | | |
| 2:00–3:00 | | | | | | | |
| 3:00–4:00 | | | | | | | |
| 4:00–5:00 | | | | | | | |
| 5:00–6:00 | | | | | | | |
| 6:00–7:00 | | | | | | | |
| 7:00–8:00 | | | | | | | |
| 8:00–9:00 | | | | | | | |
| 9:00–10:00 | | | | | | | |
| 10:00–11:00 | | | | | | | |
| 11:00–12:00 | | | | | | | |

Notes:

Care Leader's Monthly Report

# INTERCESSORY
## *Prayer*
# MINISTRY

At _____ Church we take prayer very seriously.

### THE NECESSITY OF PRAYER

For an individual or a church that desires to be used by God, prayer is not optional. It is required. We believe that meaningful and lasting results in our church can always be traced to a praying individual or group. Therefore, we try to give prayer the proper focus in our church that God gives it in His Word.

### THE INTERCESSORY PRAYER ROOM

In Isaiah 56:7 God said, "My house shall be called a house of prayer for all nations." Leviticus 6:13 says, "A fire shall always be burning on the altar; it shall never go out." Following these scriptural models, we schedule voluntary prayer warriors in our prayer room ___ hours a day, _____ days a year.

Training is provided for all intercessors. For more information about the intercessory prayer-room ministry, call [your church office's number or intercessory-prayer-room coordinator's number].

If you have a prayer request, call [your church's prayer line], and an intercessor will pray with you.

*If My people who are called by My name will humble themselves, and pray and seek My face, and turn from their wicked ways, then I will hear from heaven, and will forgive their sin and heal their land.*

2 Chronicles 7:14

### INTERCESSORY PRAYER ROOM
[Your church's name, address, and prayer line]

# PRAYER-MINISTRY BUDGET

Account name: _____ Account number: _____

**Purpose and Description**

_____

_____

_____

| Ministry | Detail | Quantity | Cost |
|----------|--------|----------|------|
|  |  |  |  |
|  |  |  | **Total** |

This year's budget: _____ Next year's proposed budget: _____ Percent change: _____

### Anticipated Monthly Disbursement of This Account

| Jan. | Feb. | Mar. | Apr. | May | June | July | Aug. | Sept. | Oct. | Nov. | Dec. |
|------|------|------|------|-----|------|------|------|-------|------|------|------|
|  |  |  |  |  |  |  |  |  |  |  |  |

Prayer-Ministry Budget Sheet

Account name: _____Prayer Ministry_____ Account number: ___00000___

## Purpose and Description

The prayer ministry exists to encourage and equip believers to fervently call on God so that the church can have His blessing in all our service to Him. We do that through four strategic prayer ministries designed to intercede for the pastor, the church body, and others.

| Ministry | Detail | Quantity | Cost* |
|---|---|---|---|
| **Pastor's prayer partners** | Newsletter/postage<br>Quarterly breakfast | 25 x 4 x .33<br>$40 x 4 | $33<br>$160 |
| **Prayer room** | Prayergrams<br>Prayer-request cards<br>Postage<br>Telephone | 1,000<br>10,000<br>1,000 x .33 | $75<br>$600<br>$330<br>$360 |
| **Annual prayer conference** | Speaker's honorarium<br>Speaker's travel<br>Speaker's hotel<br>Speaker's meals<br>Promotional mailing<br>Giveaway prizes | <br><br><br><br>500 x .33 | $250<br>$250<br>$60<br>$50<br>$165<br>$50 |
| **Intercessors' newsletter** | Paper<br>Postage | 5 reams<br>100 x 12 x .33 | $25<br>$396 |
| **Miscellaneous** | Unforeseen expenses | | $120 |
| | | **Total** | $2,924 |

This year's budget: __$2,658__  Next year's proposed budget: __$2,924__  Percent change: __10__

### Anticipated Monthly Disbursement of This Account

| Jan. | Feb. | Mar. | Apr. | May | June | July | Aug. | Sept. | Oct. | Nov. | Dec. |
|---|---|---|---|---|---|---|---|---|---|---|---|
| $149 | $171 | $126 | $449 | $101 | $101 | $149 | $266 | $761 | $449 | $101 | $101 |

*All prices are strictly for illustrative purposes.

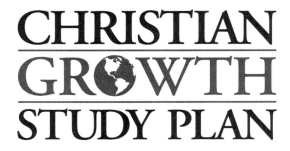

# CHRISTIAN GROWTH STUDY PLAN

In the **Christian Growth Study Plan** (formerly **Church Study Course**), this book *A House of Prayer: Prayer Ministries in Your Church* is a resource for course credit in the subject area Adult Leadership and Skill Development of the Christian Growth category of plans. To receive credit, read the book, complete the learning activities, show your work to your pastor, a staff member or church leader, then complete the following information. This page may be duplicated. Send the completed page to:

Christian Growth Study Plan
One LifeWay Plaza; Nashville, TN 37234-0117
FAX: (615)251-5067
E-mail: *cgspnet@lifeway.com*
For information about the Christian Growth Study Plan, refer to the Christian Growth Study Plan Catalog. It is located online at *www.lifeway.com/cgsp*. If you do not have access to the Internet, contact the Christian Growth Study Plan office (1.800.968.5519) for the specific plan you need for your ministry.

## *A House of Prayer: Prayer Ministries in Your Church*
### COURSE NUMBER: LS-0034

### PARTICIPANT INFORMATION

| Social Security Number (USA ONLY-optional) | Personal CGSP Number* | Date of Birth (MONTH, DAY, YEAR) |
|---|---|---|
| | | |

| Name (First, Middle, Last) | | Home Phone |
|---|---|---|
| | | |

| Address (Street, Route, or P.O. Box) | City, State, or Province | Zip/Postal Code |
|---|---|---|
| | | |

Please check appropriate box:  ❏ Resource purchased by self  ❏ Resource purchased by church  ❏ Other

### CHURCH INFORMATION

| Church Name |
|---|
| |

| Address (Street, Route, or P.O. Box) | City, State, or Province | Zip/Postal Code |
|---|---|---|
| | | |

### CHANGE REQUEST ONLY

| ☐ Former Name |
|---|
| |

| ☐ Former Address | City, State, or Province | Zip/Postal Code |
|---|---|---|
| | | |

| ☐ Former Church | City, State, or Province | Zip/Postal Code |
|---|---|---|
| | | |

| Signature of Pastor, Conference Leader, or Other Church Leader | Date |
|---|---|
| | |

*New participants are requested but not required to give SS# and date of birth. Existing participants, please give CGSP# when using SS# for the first time. Thereafter, only one ID# is required. **Mail to:** Christian Growth Study Plan, One LifeWay Plaza, Nashville, TN 37234-0117. Fax: (615)251-5067.

Rev. 3-03